For India and Pete, with love

# MEL CLARK

# KNITTING
# EVERYDAY
# FINERY

PRACTICAL DESIGNS
FOR DRESSING UP
IN LITTLE WAYS

Photography by Helen Bankers

**COLLINS & BROWN**

First published in the United Kingdom in 2012 by
Collins & Brown
10 Southcombe Street
London
W14 0RA

An imprint of Anova Books Company Ltd

Originally published in New Zealand in 2012 by
David Bateman Ltd, 30 Tarndale Grove, Albany,
Auckland www.batemanpublishing.co.nz

Text and diagrams © Mel Clark, 2012
Typographical design © David Bateman Ltd, 2012
Photographs © Helen Bankers, 2012

The moral rights of the author have been asserted.

ISBN 978-1-84340-663-1

A CIP catalogue record for this book is available from
the British Library.

10 9 8 7 6 5 4 3 2 1

Printed and bound in China through Colorcraft Ltd,
Hong Kong

This book can be ordered direct from the publisher
at www.anovabooks.com

# CONTENTS

## MY KIND OF FINERY

My first experience of feeling well-dressed came when I was six years old. My mother knitted me a cardigan for which I was allowed to choose the yarn. I decided on a cream wool with multicoloured flecks, and I watched, fascinated, as my cardigan grew, acquiring as it went insert pockets and a shawl collar. The first day it was finished, I wore it to school. I felt on top of the world, and that sense of pride when wearing a beautifully made garment has stayed with me throughout my life. Because of that experience, I have always associated hand knits with a sense of luxury.

My family was of modest means, but through my parents' hard work and ingenuity, we never felt that we lacked material things. If we did go shopping, it was most likely for fabric to make a dress or for knitting wool. My parents' best outfits lasted for years. Mum's was a linen suit that she wore to every parent conference and school event. We saved up our money, bought quality and took good care of things to make them last. My mother made many of our clothes until we were old enough to make our own. She gave me a love of handmade things, and the sense of well-being and comfort that they create in the maker and the wearer.

The word finery is often associated with fancy outfits, jewellery, lace and frippery. It can be this. My kind of finery is something more practical than that: garments or accessories that you can wear every day and enjoy because they are made with love and quality materials. Even though they are handmade, they can still have the 'wow' factor associated with fancy outfits. Many's the time I wear something handmade and get asked where I bought it. This is the ultimate compliment for a knitter: to inspire envy in non-knitters and make the world a better place by encouraging them to learn.

For this book, I've made a collection of patterns that are finery, but not just in the sense of 'dressing up in your best'. They are practical accessories that can be worn any time and, in the case of the Family Hood, by kids, too. I've included two cardigans because I have always felt that cardigans can be worn anywhere and are an essential accessory. The whimsical Daisy Dachshund pencil case is something I've wanted to make for a long time, because of a family love of dachsies and because I believe that kids need to be reminded during their school day that they are loved at home.

## CHOOSING YARNS

Which comes first, the design or the yarn? For me, the answer is the yarn.

I fall in love easily. Colours seduce me. Texture is important, too. A yarn doesn't have to feel luxurious, but it helps. I prefer natural fibres. In my experience they last longer and are more comfortable to wear. All of this contributes to the experience of the knitter and that of the person wearing the finished item.

Sometimes I will think of a design and choose a yarn to suit. Cost is an important factor. I understand that many knitters are price conscious, and for the projects in this book I have tried, for the most part, to use good-quality, natural fibres that are affordable for any budget. However, because my parents taught me to be thrifty by buying quality, I believe that it's worth paying a little more for something that will last, give pleasure and look stunning. Hand-dyed yarns are my personal favourite and for those we pay a little more. For one project in this book I have used cashmere, a luxury by any measure. I hesitated before I chose it, knowing that many might find it too expensive. The project is the Heroine Hood on page 32. It's meant to be a special garment, something you could wear every day or for an evening out. For something unique that I will use for a lifetime, I consider this money well spent.

If your budget does not permit you to buy some of the yarns I have used, it is possible to substitute others. Knowing how to do this is an essential part of the knitting experience, since yarns are sometimes discontinued. When I knit from vintage knitting patterns, most of which use yarns that are no longer available, I do a little research before I start in order to decide on the best materials. Experienced knitters do this by reading the tension and needle size. For those who are not so confident, I have included some guidelines for substituting yarns on page 122.

# Big Houndstooth Cowl

This chunky, textured scarf is made with a double strand of soft worsted yarn and is wrapped twice around the neck. The houndstooth pattern is an easy combination of knits and purls and is suitable for a beginner. Because the cowl is knit in the round, I have included instructions for knitting a swatch in rows.

## FINISHED MEASUREMENTS
Circumference: 134 cm (52 in)

Length: 25.5 cm (10 in)

## YARN
Blue Sky Alpacas Worsted [50% royal alpaca / 50% merino wool; 91 metres (100 yards) / 100 grams]: 5 hanks #2009 tan

## NEEDLES
9 mm x 80 cm (32 in) circular

Change needle size if necessary to obtain correct tension.

## NOTIONS
Jumbo stitch marker; tapestry needle

## TENSION
9.7 sts and 14.5 rnds = 10 cm (4 in) in houndstooth pattern using size 9 mm needle and 2 strands of yarn

## TENSION SWATCH (optional)
Cast on 16 sts with 2 strands of yarn.

*Work back and forth in rows as foll:*
**Row 1 (RS):** *K2, p2, k4; rep from * to end.
**Row 2:** *P4, k2, p2; rep from * to end.
**Row 3:** Rep Row 1.
**Row 4:** *K6, p2; rep from * to end.
**Row 5:** *K2, p6; rep from * to end.
**Row 6:** *P2, k6; rep from * to end.
**Row 7:** *P6, k2; rep from * to end.
**Row 8:** *P2, k2, p4; rep from * to end.
**Row 9:** *K4, p2, k2; rep from * to end.
**Row 10:** Rep Row 8.
Rep Rows 1–10 once more. Cast off.

## COWL

With 2 strands of yarn, cast on 128 sts.
Join for working in the rnd, being careful not to twist sts; pm for beg of rnd and sm on every rnd.
**Rnd 1:** *K2, p2; rep from * to end.
Rep Rnd 1 for 2x2 rib twice more.

*Commence houndstooth patt as foll:*
**Rnds 1–3:** *K2, p2, k4; rep from * to end.
**Rnds 4 & 5:** *K2, p6; rep from * to end.
**Rnds 6 & 7:** *P6, k2; rep from * to end.
**Rnds 8–10:** *K4, p2, k2; rep from * to end.
Rep Rnds 1–10 twice more.
Work 3 rnds 2x2 rib as before.
Cast off purlwise.
Using tapestry needle, weave in ends on WS.

# Barcelona Hood & Scarf

I love the dramatic effect of a lace pattern knit in a chunky yarn. Made in soft cotton to wear in springtime, this scood (scarf and hood) would also be beautiful in wool. The panels of garter stitch keep it from rolling at the edges.

## FINISHED MEASUREMENTS

Length from top of head to end of scarf (approx): 104 cm (41 in)

Hood circumference: 54.5 cm (21½ in)

## YARN

Blue Sky Alpacas Worsted Cotton [100% organically grown cotton; 137 metres (150 yards) / 100 grams]: 4 hanks #614 drift

## NEEDLES

Pair 6 mm straight

Change needle size if necessary to obtain correct tension.

## NOTIONS

Stitch holder; tapestry needle

## TENSION

15 sts and 20.5 rows = 10 cm (4 in) in chart pattern using 6 mm needles

## FIRST SCARF END

Cast on 41 sts.
Knit 3 rows (first row is WS).

*Commence working from chart as foll:*
Row 1 (RS): K4, slip 1 purlwise wyib, work 16 sts of chart twice across next 32 sts as foll — [k2tog, k4, yo, k3, yo, k4, ssk, slip 1 purlwise wyib] twice; k4.
Row 2: K4, work 16 sts of chart across next 32 sts as foll — [p6, k5, p5] twice; p1, k4.
Keeping sts either side of chart correct as set and working chart over 32 sts as established, cont until completion of Row 20 of chart, then rep Rows 1–20 a further 6 times, then Rows 1–10 once. **
Place sts onto a stitch holder.

## SECOND SCARF END

Work as for First Scarf End to **.

## Commence Hood:

With RS facing and beginning with Row 11 of chart, work as established across sts of Second Scarf End, then work as established across sts of First Scarf End, noting that there are now 8 sts in centre (former edges of scarf) in garter st – 82 sts. Keeping sts either side of chart correct as established, cont until completion of Row 20 of chart, then rep Rows 1–20 twice, then Rows 1–8 once.
Row 9: Work 37 sts, [k2tog] 4 times, work to end – 78 sts.
Row 10: Work 37 sts, cast off next 4 sts, work to end – 74 sts.

*Join top of hood:*

Break off yarn, leaving a 1.5 metre (5 foot) tail.

Place 37 sts on each needle so that tail of yarn is at point of needles.

Thread tapestry needle with yarn tail and graft sts from both needles together on RS using Kitchener Stitch (see page 126).

## FINISHING

Using tapestry needle, weave in ends on WS.

Sew cast-off sts of centre back to crown.

---

## NOTE

When working from the chart, read RS rows from right to left and WS rows from left to right.

## CHART

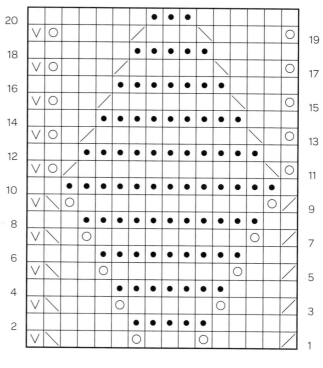

| | k on RS, p on WS | | slip 1 purlwise wyib |
|---|---|---|---|
| • | k on WS | | k2tog |
| ○ | yo | | ssk |

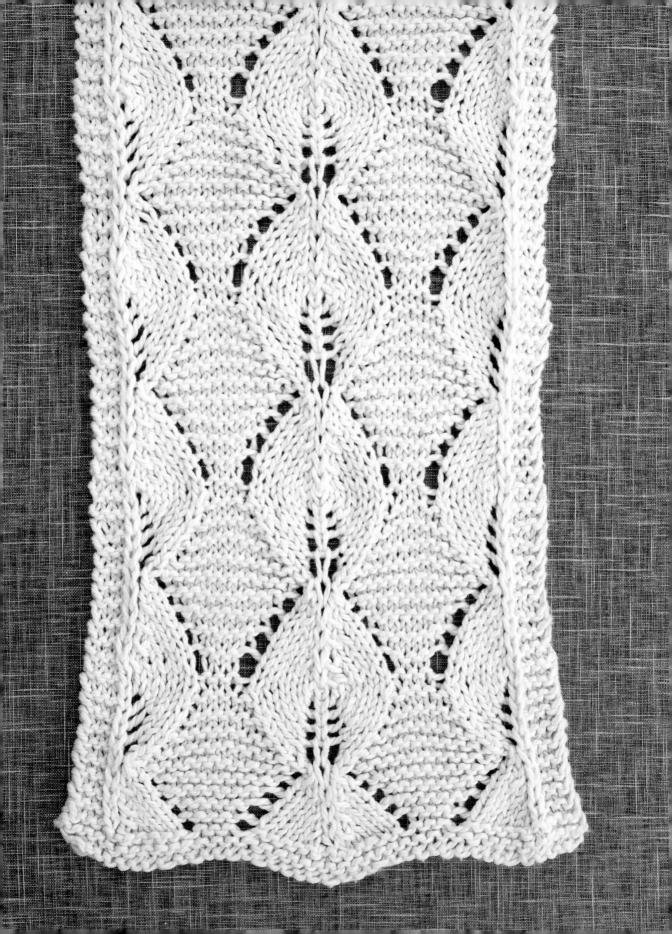

# Croissant Bag

This is a very quick knit on large needles, using four strands of worsted yarn held together. I used all of one 250-gram hank with none to spare. If your tension is different from mine, you may need a little more yarn. I made my own linen handle, which is tied through belt loops and can be made shorter if desired. A single leather store-bought handle would work well too.

## FINISHED MEASUREMENTS

Depth: 20 cm (7¾ in)

Circumference at widest point: 84 cm (33 in)

## YARN

Cascade Ecological Wool [100% wool; 437 metres (478 yards) / 250 grams]: 1 hank #8061 taupe (A)

## NEEDLES

10 mm x 60 cm (24 in) circular

Change needle size if necessary to obtain correct tension.

## NOTIONS

8 jumbo stitch markers; tapestry needle; spare yarn for casting on; 50 cm (20 in) fabric for lining; 1 metre (1 yard) iron-on interfacing; 2 belt loops; 1 metre (1 yard) linen 10 cm (4 in) wide or 1 leather handle; 46 cm (18 in) zip; sewing needle; thread or thin wool to match yarn colour

## TENSION

8 sts and 19 rows = 10 cm (4 in) in St st using size 10 mm needle and 4 strands of A

## FIRST SIDE

With spare yarn, cast on 79 sts.

With 4 strands of A, work back and forth in rows as foll:

**Row 1 (RS):** *K15, pm, k1, pm; rep from * 3 more times, knit to end.

Slip markers on every row.

**Row 2 and all WS rows:** Purl.

**Row 3:** Skp, *knit to 2 sts before marker, ssk, sm, slip 1 purlwise wyib, sm, k2tog; rep from * 3 more times, knit to last 2 sts, k2tog – 69 sts.

**Row 5:** Skp, *knit to marker, sm, slip 1 purlwise wyib, sm; rep from * 3 more times, knit to last 2 sts, k2tog – 67 sts.

**Rows 7–18:** Rep Rows 3–6 a further 3 times – 31 sts.

**Row 19:** Skp, k1, sm, slip 1 purlwise wyib, sm, *k2tog, k3, ssk, sm, slip 1 purlwise wyib, sm; rep from * twice more, k1, k2tog – 23 sts.

**Row 21:** Skp, sm, slip 1 purlwise wyib, sm, *k5, sm, slip 1 purlwise wyib, sm; rep from * twice more, k2tog – 21 sts.

**Row 23:** Skp removing marker, *sm, k2tog, k1, ssk, sm, slip 1 purlwise wyib; rep from * once more, sm, k2tog, k1, ssk, sm, k2tog removing marker – 13 sts.

**Row 25:** Skp removing marker, k2, sm, slip 1 purlwise wyib, sm, k3, sm, slip 1 purlwise wyib, sm, k2, k2tog removing marker – 11 sts. Break off yarn, thread onto tapestry needle, then draw yarn through each st. Pull up tightly and fasten off securely.

## SECOND SIDE

Remove spare yarn from cast-on edge whilst placing sts on needle.

With RS facing, work as for First Side from Row 1.

## FINISHING

Using tapestry needle, weave in ends on WS.
Allowing an extra 1 cm (½ in) overlap on all edges for seams, cut 2 pieces of lining to match the shape of the bag laid flat.
Cut 2 pieces of interfacing to match the 2 lining pieces, then press interfacing to WS of linings.
With RS facing each other, sew curved seam of lining.
Insert lining into bag with WS facing WS of bag, turning upper edges under 1 cm (½ in).
Using sewing needle and thread, sew zip along upper edges of both the bag and lining.
Attach belt loops to upper edges of bag at each end of zip.

## LINEN HANDLE

Cut a strip of interfacing the same shape as the long linen piece and iron to WS of linen. Fold lengthways with interfacing on outside, and sew along long edge and one short edge.
Turn with RS facing out. Tuck open edges to WS and sew end closed. Thread through belt loops and tie each end in place with a double knot.
For leather handle option, omit belt loops and sew handle in place at each end of zip opening.

# Quilt Sampler Tam

I love patchwork and for this tam I've taken some of my favourite quilt motifs to use in a colour pattern. I had so much fun choosing colours and making the first hat that I couldn't stop myself from making more, particularly since Koigu provides so many beautiful shades. Have fun making up your own combination.

## SIZE
To fit head (approx): 52–56 cm (20½–22 in)

## FINISHED MEASUREMENT
Rim circumference (approx): 47 cm (18½ in)

## YARN
Koigu Premium Merino KPM [100% merino wool; 160 metres (175 yards) / 50 grams]: 1 hank each #2390 (A), #1110 (B), #2190 (C)

## NEEDLES
2.75 mm x 40 cm (16 in) circular

3.25 mm x 40 cm (16 in) circular

Set of 3.25 mm double pointed

Change needle size if necessary to obtain correct tension.

## NOTIONS
6 stitch markers (1 in a contrasting colour); tapestry needle

## TENSION
28 sts and 34 rnds = 10 cm (4 in) in St st chart pattern using size 3.25 mm needles

## TAM

*Pattern note: All of A is used. Save on yarn by making the cast-on tail long enough for weaving in, but as short as possible. If your tension is looser than that of the pattern, a small amount of a second hank of A may be needed.*

With smaller circular needle and A, cast on 128 sts.

Join for working in the rnd, being careful not to twist sts; pcm for beg of rnd and sm on every rnd.

**Rnd 1:** *K1 tbl, p1; rep from * to end.

**Rnd 2:** *K1, p1; rep from * to end.

Rep Rnds 1 & 2 until work measures 3.5 cm (1½ in) from beg.

**Next rnd:** *K1, kfb; rep from * to end – 192 sts.

Change to larger circular needle and work in St st (all rnds knit) as foll:

Commence working rep of 32 sts of chart 6 times across each rnd until completion of Rnd 39 of chart.

**Rnd 40:** *Work 32, pm; rep from * 4 times more, work to end.

### Shape Crown:

*Note: Change to dpns as required.*

**Rnd 41:** *K2tog, work to 2 sts before marker, ssk, sm; rep from * 5 times more – 180 sts.

Slipping markers on every rnd, cont working from chart as established, dec as indicated until completion of Rnd 70 of chart and removing markers in last rnd – 12 sts.

Break off A, thread onto tapestry needle, then draw yarn through each st. Pull up tightly and fasten off securely.

Weave in ends on WS.

Lightly block and press to shape.

# CHART

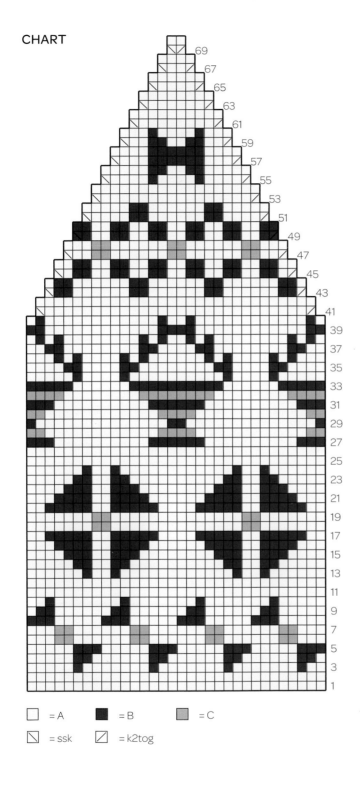

69
67
65
63
61
59
57
55
53
51
49
47
45
43
41
39
37
35
33
31
29
27
25
23
21
19
17
15
13
11
9
7
5
3
1

☐ = A   ■ = B   ▨ = C

◹ = ssk   ◿ = k2tog

## NOTES

When working from the chart, read all rnds from right to left.

When working with 2 colours, weave the float yarn around the working yarn on WS every 2 or 3 sts.

Colour choices shown in the photograph opposite are (from top to bottom):

1: 2403 (A), 2120 (B), 1193 (C)

2: 1180 (A), 2341 (B), 1055 (C)

3: 2390 (A), 1110 (B), 2190 (C)

4: 1128 (A), 2390 (B), 1043 (C)

5: 1043 (A), 2235 (B), 2390 (C)

6: 1161 (A), 2385 (B), 2341 (C)

# Family Hood

I love stripes, especially bold, wide ones. I originally designed this for children, thinking a one-piece neck warmer and hood would be easy to wear and convenient to stash in a school bag. When I saw the child's version I wanted one for myself, hence the larger sizes and possibility of hoods for the whole family. The possibilities for colour combinations are plentiful. You could choose harmonious shades as I have done, or complementary colours such as black and white, or blue and orange for a more vivid effect. Choose from two options for the ribbed edging.

## SIZES
4–6 years (8–10 years:small adult: large adult)

## FINISHED MEASUREMENTS
To fit head: 54 (55:56:59) cm [21¼ (21½:22:23¼) in]

Length (approx): 34 (38:43:47) cm [13½ (15:17:18½) in]

## YARN
Cascade 220 [100% merino wool; 201 metres (220 yards) / 100 grams]: 1 hank each A and B

or Naturally Loyal [100% wool; 105 metres (115 yards) / 50 grams]: 1 (2:2:2) skeins each A and B

## NEEDLES
4 mm x 60 cm (24 in) circular

4.5 mm x 60 cm (24 in) circular

Extra 4.5 mm needle for grafting sts

Change needle size if necessary to obtain correct tension.

## NOTIONS
3 stitch markers (1 in a contrasting colour); tapestry needle

## TENSION
20 sts and 26 rnds = 10 cm (4 in) in St st using size 4.5 mm needle

## HOOD
With smaller needle and A, cast on 112 (116:120:124) sts. Join for working in the rnd, being careful not to twist sts; pcm for beg of rnd and sm on every rnd.

*Option 1 (1x1 rib):*
**Rnd 1:** *K1, p1; rep from * to end.
Rep Rnd 1 a further 5 times.

*Option 2 (2x2 rib):*
**Rnd 1:** *K2, p2; rep from * to end.
Rep Rnd 1 a further 5 times.

*Both Options:*
Change to larger needle and work in St st as foll:
**Rnd 1:** Knit.
**Rnd 2:** *K28 (29:30:31), pm, k56 (58:60:62), pm, knit to end. Slip markers on every rnd.
**Dec rnd:** *Knit to 2 sts before marker, ssk, sm, k2tog; rep from * once more, knit to end – 108 (112:116:120) sts.
Knit 7 (9:11:13) rnds. Break off A.
Change to B and knit 3 rnds.
**Dec rnd:** *Knit to 2 sts before marker, ssk, sm, k2tog; rep from * once more, knit to end – 104 (108:112:116) sts.
Knit 8 (10:10:12) rnds.
Retaining contrasting marker, remove rem 2 markers.

### Divide for Face:
**Rnd 1:** K48 (50:52:54), cast off next 8 sts, knit to end, sm (this will now be the centre back marker), then k48 (50:52:54) sts of next rnd, turn – 96 (100:104:108) sts.

The Family Hood is shown in:
Child: Cascade 220 #9461 lime heather (A) and #9407 celery heather (B)

Woman: Cascade 220 #4146 persimmon (A) and #2451 nectarine heather (B)

Man: Naturally Loyal #905 (A) and #940 (B)

Cont in St st, working back and forth in rows as foll:
**Row 1 (WS):** P2tog, purl to last 2 sts, p2tog tbl – 94 (98:102: 106) sts.
**Row 2:** Skp, knit to last 2 sts, k2tog – 92 (96:100:104) sts.
Work 0 (0:1:1) row(s).
Dec 1 st (as before) at each end of next row – 90 (94:98:102) sts.
Work 0 (0:1:1) row(s).
Break off B.
Change to A and dec 1 st (as before) at each end of next row, then on every foll alt row 1 (1:0:0) time(s) – 86 (90:96:100) sts.
Work 1 row.

**Shape Back of Hood:**
**Row 1 (RS):** Skp, knit to 1 st before centre back marker, m1, k1, sm, k1, m1, knit to last 2 sts, k2tog – 86 (90:96:100) sts.
**Row 2:** Purl.
**Row 3:** Skp, knit to last 2 sts, k2tog – 84 (88:94:98) sts.
Rep Rows 2 & 3 a further 2 (2:3:3) times, then Row 2 once – 80 (84:88:92) sts.
**Next row:** As Row 1 – 80 (84:88:92) sts.
Rep Rows 2 & 3 a further 1 (2:2:2) time(s) – 78 (80:84:88) sts.
Work 1 (1:3:5) row(s). Break off A.
Change to B and work 16 (18:20:22) rows, dec 1 st

(as before) at each end of next row for size 4–6 years only –
76 (80:84:88) sts.
Break off B.
Change to A and work 16 (18:20:22) rows.
Break off A.
Change to B and work 1 row.

### Turn Head:
**Row 1 (WS):** P33 (35:36:38), p2tog, turn.
**Row 2:** Slip 1 purlwise wyib, knit to end.
Rep Rows 1 & 2 a further 6 (6:8:8) times.
**Next row:** P33 (35:36:38), p2tog, slide stitch just worked back
to left needle – 34 (36:37:39) sts on each end of needle.
Place one group of 34 (36:37:39) sts on a second size 7 needle.
Break off yarn, leaving a tail at least 4 times the length of sts
on one needle.
Thread tapestry needle with yarn tail and graft sts from both
needles together on RS using Kitchener Stitch (see page 126).

## FINISHING
### Face Edging:
*Option 1 (1x1 rib):*
With RS facing, smaller needle and A, pu and knit
117 (129:147:159) sts evenly around face opening, omitting
8 cast-off sts at centre front.
Work back and forth in rows as foll:
**Row 1 (WS):** *K1, p1; rep from * to last st, k1.
**Row 2:** *P1, k1; rep from * to last st, p1.
Rep Rows 1 & 2 twice more, then Row 1 once.
Cast off loosely ribwise.

*Option 2 (2x2 rib):*
With RS facing, smaller needle and A, pu and knit
116 (128:148:160) sts evenly around face opening, omitting
8 cast-off sts at centre front.
Work back and forth in rows as foll:
**Row 1 (WS):** K1, p2, *k2, p2; rep from * to last st, k1.
**Row 2:** P1, k2, *p2, k2; rep from * to last st, p1.
Rep Rows 1 & 2 twice more, then Row 1 once.
Cast off loosely ribwise.

*Both Options:*
Using tapestry needle, weave in ends on WS.
Sew side edges of ribbing in place along 8 cast-off sts at
centre front, noting that edges will overlap slightly.

# Pine Cone Mittens

These mittens are embellished with an easy slipstitch pattern inspired by the shape of spruce tree cones. I love the rustic look of this yarn, which lends itself very well to men's mittens. The pattern is on the back of the hand only, with the palms and fingers in plain stocking stitch.

## SIZES
Men's small (medium:large)

## FINISHED MEASUREMENTS
Hand circumference
(approx): 23.5 (25:26) cm
[9 1/4 (9 3/4:10 1/4) in]

Length (approx): 25 (26:26.5) cm
[10 (10 1/4:10 1/2) in]

## YARN
Manos Del Uruguay Wool
Clasica [kettle-dyed pure wool;
126 metres (138 yards) /
100 grams]: 1 hank #I quail

## NEEDLES
Set of 4.5 mm double pointed

Set of 5 mm double pointed

Change needle size if necessary
to obtain correct tension.

## NOTIONS
3 (4:5) stitch markers (1 in a
contrasting colour); scrap yarn;
tapestry needle

## TENSION
16 sts and 24 rnds = 10 cm (4 in) in
St st using size 5 mm needles

17 sts and 30 rnds = 10 cm (4 in) in
slip stitch pattern using size 5 mm
needles

## LEFT MITTEN

With smaller dpns, cast on 34 (36:38) sts, dividing evenly over 3 needles.

Join for working in the rnd, being careful not to twist sts; pcm for beg of rnd and sm on every rnd.

**Rnd 1:** *K1, p1; rep from * to end.

Rep Rnd 1 until cuff measures 9 cm (3 1/2 in).

Change to larger dpns.

**Next rnd:** Knit. **

### Shape Thumb Gusset:

Commence working from chart at Rnd 5 (3:1) as foll:

**Next rnd:** K17 (18:19), pm, m1, pm, [k1, pm] 0 (0:1) time(s), work 17 sts of Rnd 5 (3:1) of chart, [pm, k1] 0 (1:1) times – 35 (37:39) sts.

*** Slipping markers in every rnd, cont working chart between markers as established, with St st either side, as foll:

Work 2 (2:1) rnd(s).

**Next rnd:** Work 17 (18:19), sm, m1r, k1, m1l, sm, work to end – 37 (39:41) sts.

Work 2 (2:1) rnd(s).

**Next rnd:** Work 17 (18:19), sm, m1r, knit to marker, m1l, sm, work to end – 39 (41:43) sts.

Cont as established, inc 1 st (as before) inside thumb markers in every foll 3rd rnd 4 (4:5) times – 13 (13:15) sts between thumb markers and 47 (49:53) sts in all.

**Next rnd:** Removing thumb marker(s) but retaining chart markers, work 17 (18:19), thread next 13 (13:15) sts onto a piece of spare yarn, turn, cast on 1 st, turn, work to end – 35 (37:39) sts.

Work until completion of Rnd 45 of chart.

Knit 1 rnd, removing marker(s) for chart and dec 3 (1:3) st(s) evenly across rnd – 32 (36:36) sts.

## Shape Mitten Top:
**Rnd 1:** [K2, k2tog] 8 (9:9) times – 24 (27:27) sts.
**Rnd 2:** Knit.
**Rnd 3:** [K1, k2tog] 8 (9:9) times – 16 (18:18) sts.
**Rnd 4:** Knit.
**Rnd 5:** [K2tog] 8 (9:9) times – 8 (9:9) sts.
Break off yarn, thread onto tapestry needle, then draw yarn through each st. Pull up tightly and fasten off securely.

## Thumb:
Place 13 (13:15) sts from spare yarn onto larger dpns, dividing evenly over 3 needles, pu and knit 1 st into the cast-on st of hand and join for working in the rnd – 14 (14:16) sts.
Cont in St st, working in rnds until thumb measures to middle of thumb nail when fitted on hand or approx 4.5 (5:5) cm [1¾ (2:2) in] from pick-up rnd, dec 0 (0:2) sts in last rnd – 14 sts.

## Shape Thumb:
**Rnd 1:** [K2tog, k3] twice, k2tog, k2 – 11 sts.
**Rnd 2:** Knit.
**Rnd 3:** [K2tog, k2] twice, k2tog, k1 – 8 sts.
**Rnd 4:** Knit.
**Rnd 5:** [K2tog, k1] twice, k2tog – 5 sts.
Break off yarn, thread onto tapestry needle, then draw yarn through each st. Pull up tightly and fasten off securely.
Using tapestry needle, weave in ends on WS using yarn end at base of thumb to close any holes. ***

## RIGHT MITTEN
Work as for Left Mitten to **.

## Shape Thumb Gusset:
Commence working from chart at Rnd 5 (3:1) as foll:
**Next rnd:** [K1, pm] 0 (1:1) time(s), work 17 sts of Rnd 5 (3:1) of chart, [pm, k1] 0 (0:1) time(s), pm, m1, pm, k17 (18:19).
Complete as for Left Mitten from *** to ***.

## CHART

NOTE

When working from the chart, read all rnds from right to left.

|  | 45 |
|---|---|
|  | 43 |
|  | 41 |
|  | 39 |
|  | 37 |
|  | 35 |
|  | 33 |
|  | 31 |
|  | 29 |
|  | 27 |
|  | 25 |
|  | 23 |
|  | 21 |
|  | 19 |
|  | 17 |
|  | 15 |
|  | 13 |
|  | 11 |
|  | 9 |
|  | 7 |
|  | 5 —— size 1 |
|  | 3 —— size 2 |
|  | 1 —— size 3 |

☐ = knit

Ⅴ = slip 1 purlwise wyif

# Heroine Hood

This hood is shaped with short rows and decreases, and is closed in front with two buttons. You could make the neck piece longer and tie it in front if desired. I made mine in cashmere for a special gift, but you could substitute a less expensive yarn (see page 122) and the result would be just as pretty. The neck and the face edging can be made smaller if desired.

## SIZE
Women's (adjustable)

## FINISHED MEASUREMENTS
Buttoned neck circumference (approx): 44 cm (17 1/4 in) or desired width

Face edging (approx): 66 cm (26 in) or desired length

## YARN
Jade Sapphire Mongolian Cashmere 8 ply [100% cashmere; 91 metres (100 yards) / 55 grams]: 3 hanks #96 peach honey

## NEEDLES
Pair 4.5 mm straight

Pair 5 mm straight

Pair 5.5 mm straight

Change needle size if necessary to obtain correct tension.

## NOTIONS
3 stitch markers; tapestry needle; two 2 cm (3/4 in) buttons; contrasting thread for finishing

## TENSION
17 sts and 23 rows = 10 cm (4 in) in St st using size 5.5 mm needles

## HOOD

With 5 mm needles, cast on 112 sts.
Work 3 rows St st, beg with a purl row.
Change to largest needles.

**Commence Short Rows:**
**Row 1 (RS):** Knit to last 4 sts, turn.
**Row 2:** Slip 1 purlwise, purl to last 4 sts, turn.
**Row 3:** Slip 1 knitwise, knit to last 8 sts, turn.
**Row 4:** Slip 1 purlwise, purl to last 8 sts, turn.
**Row 5:** Slip 1 knitwise, k96, turn.
**Row 6:** Slip 1 purlwise, p97, turn.
**Row 7:** Slip 1 knitwise, k101, turn.
**Row 8:** Slip 1 purlwise, p105, turn.
**Row 9:** Slip 1 knitwise, knit to end.
**Row 10:** Purl.
**Row 11:** Knit.
**Row 12:** Purl.
Rep Rows 1–12 once more, then Rows 1–11 once.
**Next row:** *P28, pm; rep from * twice, purl to end.
**Next row:** Skp, *knit to 2 sts before marker, k2tog, sm, ssk; rep from * twice, knit to last 2 sts, k2tog – 104 sts.
**Next row:** Purl, slipping markers.
Rep last 2 rows 11 times more – 16 sts.
**Next row:** Skp, *k2tog, remove marker, ssk; rep from * twice, k2tog – 8 sts.
**Next row:** Purl.
**Next row:** [Skp] twice, [k2tog] twice – 4 sts.
Cast off.

*NOTE: Cast-on edge is face edge of hood. Side edge is neck edge of hood.*

## FACE EDGING

With 5 mm needles, cast on 13 sts.
**Row 1 (WS):** Purl.
**Row 2:** K6, slip 1 purlwise wyib, k6.
Rep Rows 1 & 2 until piece measures 66 cm (26 in) or desired length, ending with Row 2.
Cast off purlwise.

## NECK BAND

With smallest needles, cast on 15 sts.
**Row 1 (RS):** [P1, k1] 7 times, p1.
**Row 2:** [K1, p1] 7 times, k1.
Rep Rows 1 & 2 once more.
**Buttonhole row:** [P1, k1] twice, yo, k2tog, [p1, k1] twice, yo, k2tog, p1, k1, p1.
**Next row:** As Row 2.
Rep Rows 1 & 2 until piece measures 46.5 cm (18¼ in) or 2.5 cm (1 in) more than desired finished neck circumference, ending with Row 2.
Cast off knitwise.

## FINISHING

Using tapestry needle, weave in ends on WS.
With RS facing each other, thread tapestry needle with contrasting thread and tack one edge of face edging to cast-on edge of hood, easing into place. Sew in place on WS, then remove tacking stitches.
Fold Face Edging to WS along centre slip sts and sew to WS of hood, easing face edge of hood into place.
With buttonholes at right face edge, sew long edge of Neck Band to neck edge of hood on WS, easing hood edge into place and leaving 2.5 cm (1 in) at each end of Neck Band for button overlap.
Sew buttons in place to correspond with buttonholes.

# Strawberry Beret

This is a quick knit in a thick sumptuous yarn using a textured stitch pattern. The pattern is formed by purling and knitting the same three stitches together three times. Both sides of the pattern are equally attractive. You can choose which side to show.

## SIZES
Women's small (medium/large)

To fit head (approx):
53–55 (56–59) cm
[21–21½ (22–23¼) in]

## FINISHED MEASUREMENTS
Rim circumference:
49.5 (53.5) cm
[19½ (21) in]

## YARN
Blue Sky Alpacas Worsted
[50% royal alpaca / 50% merino wool; 91 metres (100 yards) / 100 grams]: 2 hanks #2018 strawberry

## NEEDLES
5 mm x 40 cm (16 in) circular

6 mm x 40 cm (16 in) circular

Set of 6 mm double pointed

Change needle size if necessary to obtain correct tension.

## NOTIONS
Stitch marker; tapestry needle

## TENSION
17 sts and 16 rnds = 10 cm (4 in) in patt using size 6 mm needles

## BERET

With smaller circular needle, cast on 66 (72) sts.
Join for working in the rnd, being careful not to twist sts; pm for beg of rnd and sm on every rnd.
**Rnd 1:** *K1 tbl, p1; rep from * to end.
**Rnd 2:** *K1, p1; rep from * to end.
Rep Rnd 2 until piece measures 3 cm (1¼ in) from beg.
**Inc rnd:** *K1, kfb; rep from * to end – 99 (108) sts.
**Next rnd:** Knit, inc 9 (4) sts evenly across – 108 (112) sts.
Change to larger circular needle.

*Commence patt as foll:*
**Rnd 1:** *[P3tog, yb, knit the same 3 sts tog, yf, purl the same 3 sts tog], k1; rep from * to end.
**Rnd 2:** Knit.
**Rnd 3:** K2, *[p3tog, yb, knit the same 3 sts tog, yf, purl the same 3 sts tog], k1; rep from * to last 2 sts, k2.
**Rnd 4:** Knit.
Rep Rnds 1–4 until piece measures 18 cm (7 in) from cast-on edge, ending Rnd 3.

**Shape Crown:**
*NOTE: Change to dpns as required.*

*Size Small Only:*
**Next rnd:** *K2, k2tog; rep from * to last 4 sts, [k2tog] twice – 80 sts.
Rep Rnds 1–3 of patt.
**Next rnd:** *K2, k2tog; rep from * to end – 60 sts.
***Rep Rnds 1–3 of patt.
**Next rnd:** *K1, k2tog; rep from * to end – 40 sts.
Rep Rnd 1 of patt.
**Next rnd:** *K2tog; rep from * to end – 20 sts.
Rep Rnd 1 of patt.
**Next rnd:** *K2tog; rep from * to end – 10 sts.
Rep Rnd 1 of patt. ***

*Size Medium/Large Only:*
**Next rnd:** *K2, k2tog; rep from * to end – 84 sts.
Rep Rnds 1–3 of patt.
**Next rnd:** *[K2, k2tog] 6 times, [k2tog] twice; rep from * twice more – 60 sts.
Complete as for Size Small from *** to ***.

## FINISHING

Break off yarn, thread onto tapestry needle, then draw yarn through each st. Pull up tightly and fasten off securely.
Weave in ends on WS.

# Tweed Hat & Scarf

Whenever I ask my husband what he wants me to knit for him, his request is usually for something plain, without too much detail. Since I'm the one doing the knitting, I sometimes sneak in a little extra interest for myself by using stitch patterns like these two, which complement each other. The hat is long enough so that it can be folded back at the brim.

## SIZES
Adult's small (medium/large)

To fit head: 48–53 (56–61) cm [19–21 (22–24) in]

## FINISHED MEASUREMENTS
Rim circumference: 51 (57) cm [20 (20½) in]

## YARN
Naturally Heather [100% New Zealand wool; 100 metres (109 yards) / 50 grams]: 2 balls #203

## NEEDLES
4 mm x 40 cm (16 in) circular

4.5 mm x 40 cm (16 in) circular

Set of 4.5 mm double pointed

Change needle size if necessary to obtain correct tension.

## NOTIONS
6 stitch markers (1 in a contrasting colour); tapestry needle

## TENSION
20 sts and 26 rnds = 10 cm (4 in) in patt using size 4.5 mm needles

## HAT
With smaller circular needle, cast on 102 (114) sts.
Join for working in the rnd, being careful not to twist sts; pcm for beg of rnd and sm on every rnd.

*Commence patt as foll:*
**Rnd 1:** *K5, p1; rep from * to end.
Rep Rnd 1 a further 5 times.
Change to larger circular needle and cont in patt until piece measures 19 (21) cm [7½ (8¼) in] from cast-on edge.
**Next rnd:** Work 17 (19), *pm, work 17 (19); rep from * to end.

## Shape Crown:
*NOTE: Change to dpns as required.*
**Dec rnd:** *K2tog, work to 2 sts before marker, ssk, sm; rep from * to end – 90 (102) sts.
Work 1 rnd, slipping markers.
Rep last 2 rnds until 18 sts rem.
**Dec rnd:** *K2tog, k1, remove marker; rep from * to end – 12 sts.
Break off yarn and thread onto tapestry needle, then draw yarn through each st. Pull up tightly and fasten off securely.
Weave in ends on WS.

## FINISHED MEASUREMENTS

Width: 19 cm (7 ½ in)

Length: 150 cm (59 in)

## YARN

Naturally Heather [100% New
Zealand wool; 100 metres
(109 yards) / 50 grams]:
4 balls #203

## NEEDLES

Pair 4.5 mm straight

Change needle size if necessary
to obtain correct tension.

## NOTIONS

Tapestry needle

## TENSION

24 sts and 24 rows = 10 cm (4 in)
in patt using size 4.5 mm needles

## SCARF

With straight needles, cast on 46 sts.

*Commence patt as foll:*
**Row 1:** K2, *p2, k2; rep from * to end.
**Row 2:** P2, *k2, p2; rep from * to end.
**Row 3:** Knit.
**Row 4:** Purl.
**Rows 5 & 6:** Rep Rows 1 & 2 once.
**Row 7:** Purl.
**Row 8:** Knit.
Rep Rows 1–8 until piece measures 150 cm (59 in) or desired
length, ending with Row 8.
Rep Rows 1 & 2 once.
Cast off in patt.
Using tapestry needle, weave in ends on WS.

# H@T

This double-layered hat has a striped lining to contrast with the curves of the colour work on the outside. The finished circumference is for the outer layer. The inside circumference is slightly smaller because of the space taken up by the lining. When working from the chart, twist the carried yarn around the working yarn every two or three stitches to avoid puckering.

## SIZES
To fit (approx): 43–51 (53–61) cm [17–20 (21–24) in] head circumference

## FINISHED MEASUREMENTS
Circumference (approx): 48 (58) cm [19 (23) in]

Height (approx): 24 (28) cm [9½ (11) in]

## YARN
Koigu Premium Merino KPM [100% merino wool; 160 metres (175 yards) / 50 grams]: 1 (2) hanks #2403 (A), 1 (1) hank each #2390 (B) and #1128 (C)

## NEEDLES
2.75 mm x 40 cm (16 in) circular

3 mm x 40 cm (16 in) circular

Set of 2.75 mm double pointed

Set of 3 mm double pointed

Change needle size if necessary to obtain correct tension.

## NOTIONS
5 (6) stitch markers (1 in a contrasting colour); tapestry needle; spare yarn for casting on

## TENSION
29 sts and 41 rnds = 10 cm (4 in) in St st using size 2.75 mm needles

29 sts and 43 rnds = 10 cm (4 in) in St st Fair Isle patt using size 3 mm needles

## OUTER LAYER

With smaller circular needle and spare yarn, cast on 140 (168) sts.

Join for working in the rnd, being careful not to twist sts; pcm for beg of rnd and sm on every rnd.

With larger circular needle and A, work 4 rnds St st.

Commence working 14 sts of Chart A in St st 10 (12) times across every rnd as foll:

Work Rnds 17–32 0 (1) times, Rnds 1–32 twice, then Rnds 1–13 once.

**Rnd 14:** [Work 28, pm] 4 (5) times, work 28.

### Shape Top:
*NOTE: Change to size 3 dpns as required.*

Commence working from Chart B, slipping markers on every rnd, as foll:

**Rnd 1:** With A, [k2tog, knit to 2 sts before marker, ssk, sm] 5 (6) times – 130 (156) sts.

Cont working chart between markers in St st until completion of Rnd 22 of chart – 10 (12) sts.

Break off yarn, thread onto tapestry needle, then remove markers whilst drawing yarn through each st. Pull up tightly and fasten off securely.

Using tapestry needle, weave in ends on WS.

## LINING

Remove spare yarn from cast-on edge whilst placing sts on size 2 circular needle.

Join for working in the rnd; pcm for beg of rnd and sm on every rnd.

Weaving in ends as you knit, work in St st stripes as foll:

With C, work 34 (41) rnds.

Change to A and work 24 (29) rnds.
Change to C and work 11 (13) rnds.
Change to A and work 10 (13) rnds.
**Next rnd:** [K28, pm] 4 (5) times, k28.

**Shape Top:**
Shape top same as for Outer Layer, working in A only (omitting Fair Isle) and slipping all markers on every rnd. Break off yarn, thread onto tapestry needle, then remove markers whilst drawing yarn through each st. Pull up tightly and fasten off securely, using end of yarn to sew top of lining to the top of outer layer to secure.

## CHART A

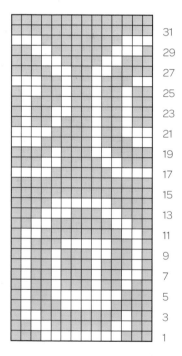

## CHART B

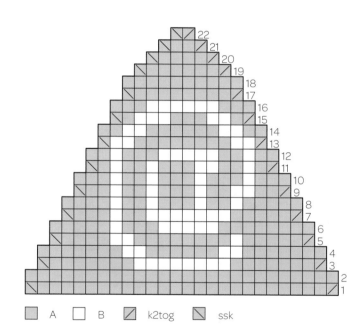

| | A | | B | | k2tog | | ssk |

## NOTES

When working from the charts, read all rnds from right to left.

To avoid long floats when working from the chart with two colours twist the carried yarn around the working yarn on WS every second stitch.

# Paisley Cuffs

Paisley is one of my favourite motifs, and it's a design that features in the textiles of many different cultures. The yarn for these cuffs was bought on a whim when I found myself unable to resist its opulent colours and rustic look. It remained in my stash, much fondled and admired, for some time before I decided what to make with it. This simple pattern is an ideal beginner intarsia project.

## SIZE
One size, to fit hand: 19 cm (7½ in)

## FINISHED MEASUREMENTS
Length: 22 cm (8¾ in)

Circumference: 20 cm (7¾ in)

## YARN
The Fibre Company Terra [40% baby alpaca / 40% wool / 20% silk; 90 metres (98 yards) / 50 grams]: 2 hanks acorn (A) and 1 hank henna (B)

## NEEDLES
Pair 4.5 mm straight

Change needle size if necessary to obtain correct tension.

## NOTIONS
4 stitch markers; tapestry needle

## TENSION
18 sts and 26 rows = 10 cm (4 in) in intarsia pattern using size 4.5 mm (US 7) needles

## LEFT CUFF

Cut six 2-metre (7 foot) lengths of B for intarsia motifs.

With A, cast on 34 sts.

Work 4 rows St st, beg with a purl row.

Knit 1 row (fold line).

Work 3 rows St st, beg with a knit row, inc 2 sts evenly across last row – 36 sts.

**Next row:** P4, pm, p10, pm, p8, pm, p10, pm, p4.

*Commence working from Chart A as foll*:

**Row 1 (RS):** K4 A, *sm, work Row 1 from Chart A as foll: k4 A, k3 B, k3 A, sm*; k8 A, rep from * to * once, k4 A.

Slipping markers on every row, cont working chart between markers as established, with St st either side, as foll:

Work until completion of Row 48 of chart, removing markers on last row.

Work 4 rows St st, beg with a knit row.

Purl 1 row (fold line).

Work 4 rows St st, beg with a purl row.

Cast off purlwise.

## RIGHT CUFF

Work as for Left Cuff, working from Chart B instead of Chart A and working Row 1 of chart as foll:

**Row 1 (RS):** K4 A, *sm, work Row 1 from Chart B as foll: k3 A, k3 B, k4 A, sm*; k8 A, rep from * to * once, k4 A.

## FINISHING

Using tapestry needle, weave in ends on WS.

Sew side seams. Turn cast-on and cast-off edges to WS along fold lines and sew in place.

## NOTES

When working from the charts, read RS rows from right to left and WS rows from left to right.

When working intarsia pattern, introduce B where required and weave yarn A around yarn B on WS every 2 sts. Do not carry B across all sts.

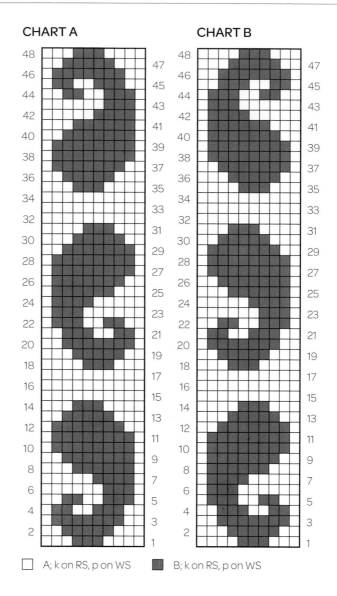

**CHART A**  **CHART B**

☐ A; k on RS, p on WS  ■ B; k on RS, p on WS

# Anna's Hair Band

I made this for a friend who often wears — and looks lovely in — a hair band. This alpaca/silk blend happens to be her favourite yarn and she introduced me to its charms. The hair band ties at the nape of the neck. It would look pretty tied under a ponytail, or with short hair.

## FINISHED MEASUREMENTS
Width: 10 cm (4 in)

Length: 89.5 cm (35¼ in)

## YARN
Blue Sky Alpaca Silk [50% alpaca / 50% silk; 133 metres (146 yards) / 50 grams]: 1 hank #141 peapod

## NEEDLES
Pair 3.25 mm straight

Pair 3.5 mm straight

Change needle size if necessary to obtain correct tension.

## NOTIONS
Tapestry needle

## TENSION
21 sts and 32 rows = 10 cm (4 in) in Lace Pattern using size 3.5 mm (US 4) needles

21 sts and 35 rows = 10 cm (4 in) in garter stitch using size 3.25 mm (US 3) needles

## NOTE
When working from the chart, read RS rows from right to left and WS rows from left to right.

## HAIR BAND

With smaller needles, cast on 185 sts.

Knit 8 rows.

**Next Row (RS):** Cast off 40 sts, knit to last 40 sts, cast off 40 sts.

Fasten off.

Change to larger needles.

With WS facing, rejoin yarn to rem 105 sts and purl to end.

*Commence working from chart as foll:*

**Row 1 (RS):** K1, ssk, knit to last 3 sts, k2tog, k1 – 103 sts.

**Row 2:** P1, p2tog, purl to last 3 sts, p2tog tbl, p1 – 101 sts.

**Row 3:** K1, ssk, k8, k2tog, yo, k3, yo, ssk, k2, [k3, k2tog, yo, k3, yo, ssk, k2] 5 times, k3, k2tog, yo, k3, yo, ssk, k8, k2tog, k1 – 99 sts.

Cont working from chart as established until completion of Row 20 – 65 sts.

Break off yarn.

With RS facing and smaller needles, pu and knit 21 sts evenly along right-slanted edge of head band; work across 65 sts of top of hair band as foll: k1, ssk, k59, k2tog, k1; then pu and knit 21 sts evenly along left-slanted edge of hair band – 105 sts.

Knit 7 rows, inc 1 st at each end of second row, then on every foll alt row – 113 sts.

Cast off.

## FINISHING

Using tapestry needle, weave in ends on WS.

Sew shaped ends of upper garter stitch edging in place to upper edge of ties.

Lightly block.

## CHART

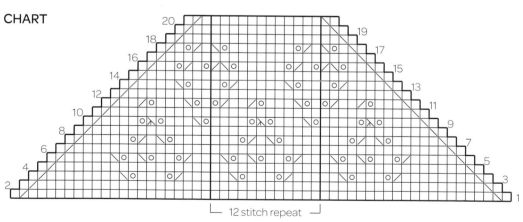

⌞ 12 stitch repeat ⌝

◿ k2tog on RS, p2tog on WS     ☐ k on RS, p on WS     ⋌ sk2p

◺ ssk on RS, p2tog tbl on WS     ⊙ yo

# Flying Geese Mitts

When I charted the cable pattern on these fingerless mitts, it reminded me of a flock of birds flying in formation. I made them in two lengths: one long, with an extended cable for a dressy look (Version A Mitts), the other short and more casual (Version B Mitts).

## SIZES
Medium (large)

## FINISHED MEASUREMENTS
Hand circumference (approx): 18.5 (20.5) cm [7¼ (8) in]

Version A length (approx): 24 cm (9½ in)

Version B length (approx): 20.5 cm (8 in)

## YARN
Cascade 220 [100% merino wool; 201 metres (220 yards) / 100 grams]: 1 hank #9559 indigo frost heather (A) or #2451 nectarine heather (B)

## NEEDLES
Set of 4 mm double pointed

Set of 4.5 mm double pointed

Change needle size if necessary to obtain correct tension.

## NOTIONS
5 stitch markers (1 in a contrasting colour); cable needle; spare yarn; tapestry needle

## TENSION
21 sts and 27 rnds = 10 cm (4 in) in St st using size 4.5 mm needles

## VERSION A MITTS

### Left Mitt:
With smaller dpns, cast on 40 (44) sts, dividing evenly over 3 needles.

Join for working in the rnd, being careful not to twist sts; pcm for beg of rnd and sm on every rnd.

**Rnd 1:** *K1, p1; rep from * to end.

Rep Rnd 1 a further 7 times for cuff. **

Change to larger dpns.

**Next rnd:** K22 (25), pm, k16, pm, k2 (3).

### Commence working from Chart A as foll:
**Rnd 1:** K22 (25), sm, k10, C4B, k2, sm, k2 (3).

Slipping markers on every rnd, cont working chart between markers as established, with St st on either side as foll:

Work until completion of Rnd 16 of chart.

**Rnd 17:** K5 (6), k2tog, k6, k2tog, work to end – 38 (42) sts.

Work until completion of Rnd 28 of chart.

### Shape Thumb:
**Rnd 29:** Work 19 (21), pm, m1, pm, work to end – 39 (43) sts.

Work 2 (1) rnd(s).

**Next rnd:** Work 19 (21), sm, m1r, knit to marker, m1l, sm, work to end – 41 (45) sts.

Work 2 (1) rnd(s).

**Next rnd:** Work 19 (21), sm, m1r, knit to marker, m1l, sm, work to end – 43 (47) sts.

Cont as established, inc 1 st (as before) inside thumb markers on every foll 3rd (2nd) rnd a further 3 (1) time(s), then on every foll 4th (3rd) rnd a further 1 (5) time(s) – 13 (17) sts between thumb markers and 51 (59) sts in all.

**Next rnd:** Work 19 (21), remove marker, thread next 13 (17) sts onto a piece of spare yarn, turn, cast 1 st, turn, remove marker, work to end – 39 (43) sts.

Work until completion of Rnd 54 of chart.

Knit 1 rnd, removing markers for chart and dec 1 st over the cable – 38 (42) sts.
Change to smaller dpns and work 4 rnds 1x1 rib as for cuff.
Cast off ribwise.

*Thumb:*
Place 13 (17) sts from spare yarn onto larger dpns, dividing evenly over 3 needles; pu and knit 1 st into the cast-on st of hand and join for working in the rnd – 14 (18) sts.
Knit 2 (3) rnds.
Change to smaller dpns and work 3 rnds 1x1 rib as for cuff.
Cast off ribwise.
Using tapestry needle, weave in ends on WS using yarn end at base of thumb to close any holes.

### Right Mitt:
Work as for Left Mitt to **.
Change to larger dpns.
**Next rnd:** K2 (3), pm, k16, pm, k22 (25).

*Commence working from Chart B as foll:*
**Rnd 1:** K2 (3), sm, k2, C4F, k10, sm, k22 (25).
Slipping markers on every rnd, cont working chart between markers as established, with St st on either side as foll:
Work until completion of Rnd 16 of chart.
**Rnd 17:** Work 25 (28), k2tog, k6, k2tog, k5 (6) – 38 (42) sts.
Work until completion of Rnd 28 of chart.

*Shape Thumb:*
Shape thumb same as for Left Mitt.

## VERSION B MITTS

### Left Mitt:
With smaller dpns, cast on 38 (42) sts, dividing evenly over 3 needles.
Join for working in the rnd, being careful not to twist sts; pcm for beg of rnd and sm on every rnd.
**Rnd 1:** *K1, p1; rep from * to end.
Rep Rnd 1 until cuff measures 8 cm (3¼ in). **
Change to larger dpns.
**Next rnd:** K20 (23), pm, k16, pm, k2 (3).
Commence working from Chart A at Rnd 23 as foll:
**Rnd 23:** K20 (23), sm, k1, C4F, k11, sm, k2 (3).
Slipping markers on every rnd, cont working chart between markers as established, with St st on either side as foll:
Work until completion of Rnd 28 of chart.

*Shape Thumb:*
Shape thumb same as for Left Mitt of Version A.

**Right Mitt:**
Work as for Left Mitt to **.
Change to larger dpns.
**Next rnd:** K2 (3), pm, k16, pm, k20 (23).
Commence working from Chart B at Rnd 23 as foll:
**Rnd 23:** K2 (3), sm, k11, C4B, k1, sm, k20 (23).
Slipping markers on every rnd, cont working chart between markers as established, with St st on either side, as foll:
Work until completion of Rnd 28 of chart.

*Shape Thumb:*
Shape thumb same as for Left Mitt of Version A.

## NOTES
When working from the charts, read all rnds from right to left.

## CHART A

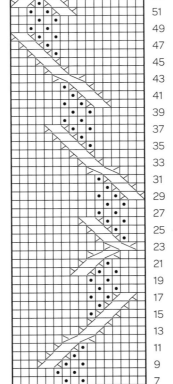

## CHART B

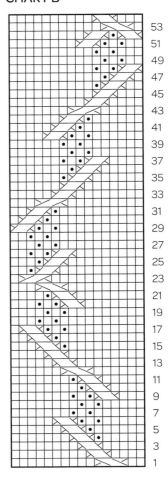

☐ knit

⊡ purl

▱ C3B: sl 1 st to cn and hold at back, k2, then k1 from cn

◺ C3F: sl 2 sts to cn and hold at front, k1, then k2 from cn

▱ C4B: sl 2 sts to cn and hold at back, k2, then k2 from cn

◺ C4F: sl 2 sts to cn and hold at front, k2, then k2 from cn

# Basket Purse

I made this purse to show off a favourite shade of multicoloured yarn. The handle is folded over, lined with lightweight cardboard to keep its shape and stitched into place around the opening. The bag is knit from the top down, in the round. Choose a pretty fabric for the bag lining.

## FINISHED MEASUREMENTS
Entrelac section: 26 cm (10¼ in) wide x 12 cm (4¾ in) high; circumference 52 cm (20½ in)

Handles: 24 cm (9½ in) wide x 7 cm (2¾ in) high

## YARN
Koigu Painter's Palette Premium Merino KPPPM [100% merino wool; 160 metres (175 yards) / 50 grams]: 2 hanks #P210

## NEEDLES
3.25 mm x 40 cm (16 in) circular

Change needle size if necessary to obtain correct tension.

## NOTIONS
3.25 mm crochet hook (optional); 4 stitch markers (1 in a contrasting colour); tapestry needle; cable needle; stitch holder; two 23 x 5.5 cm (9 x 2¼ in) pieces of thin cardboard; 50 cm (19¾ in) fabric for lining; 30 cm (11¾ in) iron-on interfacing; sewing needle; thread to match lining; contrasting thread for finishing

## TENSION
28 sts and 30 rnds = 10 cm (4 in) in St st using size 3.25 mm needle

*Special abbreviation:* P3Ctog (over 3 sts) = Slip next st to cable needle and hold to front, slip next st purlwise to right needle, slip st on cable needle back to left needle, then p2tog, psso – 1 st rem.

## PURSE

(Commence at handles)
Cast on 130 sts. Join for working in the rnd, being careful not to twist sts; pcm for beg of rnd and sm on every rnd.

*Commence Handle Lining:*
**Rnd 1:** P1, pm, k64, pm, p1, pm, k64.
**Rnd 2:** *Sm, p1, sm, knit to marker; rep from * to end.
Rep Rnd 2 for patt, slipping markers on every rnd as foll:
Work 6 rnds.
** **Rnd 9:** *Work 17, cast off next 32 sts, work 16 (including st on right needle after cast-off); rep from * to end.
Keeping patt correct, work back and forth in rows, working sts on WS rows knit and purl as they face you, as foll:
**Row 1 (RS):** Work 17, turn.
**Row 2:** Work 33, turn.
Work 7 rows on these 33 sts, thus ending with a RS row.
Break off yarn.
With RS facing, join yarn to rem 33 sts and work 9 rows, thus ending with a RS row. Turn work.
**Next row:** Cast on 32 sts purlwise over cast-off sts, turn, work 33, turn, cast on 32 sts purlwise over cast-off sts, turn, work to next marker. This now marks beg of rnd – 130 sts.
Work 8 rnds. ***
Purl 1 rnd (fold line).

*Commence Outer Layer of Handle:*
**Rnd 1:** Knit, slipping markers.
**Rnd 2:** *Sm, slip 1 purlwise, sm, knit to marker; rep from * to end.
Rep Rnds 1 & 2 for patt, slipping markers on every rnd as foll:

Work 6 rnds.
Rep from ** to ***, maintaining patt as set and noting to work WS rows as purl.

*Commence Entrelac:*
Purl 3 rnds, removing all markers.
K3, pm for beg of rnd.

**Base Triangles:**
*First Triangle:*
**Row 1 (RS):** K1, turn.
**Row 2:** P1, turn.
**Row 3:** Slip 1 purlwise wyib, k1, turn.
**Row 4 and all WS rows:** Purl all sts worked on last row, turn.
**Row 5:** Slip 1 purlwise wyib, k2, turn.
**Row 7:** Slip 1 purlwise wyib, k3, turn.
**Row 9:** Slip 1 purlwise wyib, k4, turn.
**Row 11:** Slip 1 purlwise wyib, k5, turn.
**Row 13:** Slip 1 purlwise wyib, k6, turn.
**Row 15:** Slip 1 purlwise wyib, k7, turn.
**Row 17:** Slip 1 purlwise wyib, k8, turn.
**Row 19:** Slip 1 purlwise wyib, k9. Do not turn work.

*2nd–13th Triangles:*
Work as for First Triangle – 130 sts, 10 sts in each triangle.

**Tier 1:**
*First Rectangle:*
**Row 1 (RS):** Pu and knit 10 sts along selvedge edge of next triangle, inserting needle under both threads of selvedge st, turn.
**Row 2:** Slip 1 purlwise wyif, p8, p2tog, turn.
**Row 3:** K10, turn.
**Rows 4–19:** Rep last 2 rows a further 8 times.
**Row 20:** As Row 2. Do not turn work.

*2nd Rectangle:*
**Row 1 (WS):** Pu and purl 10 sts along selvedge edge of next triangle as foll: *Insert tip of right needle under both threads of selvedge st from back to front, wrap yarn around the needle purlwise and pull through a loop; rep from * 9 times more, slip last picked up st to left needle, then p2tog.
**Row 2:** K10, turn.
**Row 3:** Slip 1 purlwise wyif, p8, p2tog, turn.
**Rows 4–19:** Rep last 2 rows a further 8 times. Do not turn work at end of Row 19.

### 3rd–13th Rectangles:

Work as for 2nd Rectangle.

### Tier 2:

*First Rectangle:*

**Row 1 (WS):** Pu and purl 10 sts along selvedge edge of next rectangle, turn.

**Row 2:** Slip 1 purlwise wyib, k8, ssk, turn.

**Row 3:** P10, turn.

**Rows 4–19:** Rep last 2 rows a further 8 times.

**Row 20:** As Row 2. Do not turn work.

*2nd Rectangle:*

**Row 1 (RS):** Pu and knit 10 sts along selvedge edge of next rectangle. Slip first st on left needle to right needle, insert left needle into last 2 sts on right needle and knit tog, turn.

**Row 2:** P10, turn.

**Row 3:** Slip 1 purlwise wyib, k8, ssk, turn.

**Rows 4–19:** Rep last 2 rows a further 8 times. Do not turn work at end of Row 19.

*3rd–13th Rectangles:*

Work as for 2nd Rectangle.

### Tiers 3 and 4:

Rep Tiers 1 and 2, picking up sts along selvedge edge of rectangles.

### Final Tier Triangles:

*First Triangle:*

**Row 1 (RS):** Pu and knit 10 sts along selvedge edge of next rectangle, turn.

**Row 2:** P9, p2tog, turn.

**Row 3:** K9, wrap, turn.

**Row 4:** P8, p2tog, turn.

**Row 5:** K8, wrap, turn.

**Row 6:** P7, p2tog, turn.

Cont as established, dec 1 st on every foll alt row until the row 'k1, wrap, turn' has been worked.

**Row 20:** P2tog, turn.

**Row 21:** Wrap, turn.

*2nd Triangle:*

**Row 1 (WS):** Pu and purl 10 sts along selvedge edge of next rectangle. Slip last picked up st to left needle, then p2tog, turn.

**Row 2:** K9, wrap, turn.

**Row 3:** P8, p2tog, turn.
**Row 4:** K8, wrap, turn.
**Row 5:** P7, p2tog, turn.
Cont as established, dec 1 st on every foll alt row until the row 'k1, wrap, turn' has been worked.
**Row 19:** P2tog, turn.
**Row 20:** Wrap, turn.

*3rd–13th Triangles:*
Work as for 2nd Triangle – 130 sts.

### Base:
Work in rnds on WS of fabric as foll:
**Rnd 1:** Purling each wrapped st tog with the wrap, p4, pcm for beg of rnd, p7, pm, p58, pm, p7, pm, p58 – 130 sts.
**Rnd 2:** *Sm, p2tog, p3, p2tog tbl, sm, purl to marker; rep from * to end – 126 sts.
**Rnd 3:** Purl, slipping markers.
**Rnd 4:** *Sm, p2tog, p1, p2tog tbl, sm, purl to marker; rep from * to end – 122 sts.
**Rnd 5:** *Remove marker, P3Ctog, remove marker, cast off st just worked, purl to marker; rep from * to end – 116 sts.
Break off yarn, leaving a 1 metre (3 foot) tail of yarn.
Thread tapestry needle with yarn tail and graft base sts together on RS using Kitchener Stitch (see page 126).

### FINISHING

Using tapestry needle, weave in ends on WS.
Block entrelac and handle section.
Cut 4 pieces of interfacing (1 for each side of handles), each with a rectangular hole to correspond with size of gap in handle section and iron to WS of each handle section.
Cut 2 pieces of cardboard (1 for each handle insert), making the cardboard 5 mm (¼ in) smaller than the handle areas on all edges, including the rectangular holes.
Fold each handle section over cardboard insert at fold line.
With a contrasting thread and tapestry needle, tack around the edges of the rectangles to hold in place.

**Edging:** Can be worked with either a crochet hook using sl st, or a tapestry needle using chain st.
With RS facing, work through double fabric around rectangular gap of each handle. Remove tacking thread.

**Lining:** Cut 1 piece of fabric 13 mm (½ in) wider and twice the length of the entrelac section. Fold in half horizontally and sew side seams.

Place lining inside bag with WS of lining facing WS of entrelac. Using a sewing needle and thread, sew in place around top of entrelac section, with handle lining overlapping fabric. Sew around the base of the handle lining to finish and hold in place.

## CHART

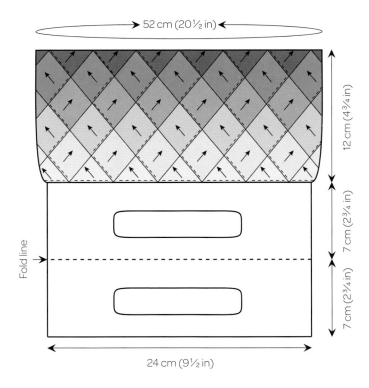

52 cm (20½ in)

12 cm (4¾ in)

7 cm (2¾ in)

7 cm (2¾ in)

Fold line

24 cm (9½ in)

Pick up sts for each tier along the edge indicated by the dotted lines. Work progresses in the direction of each arrow.

# July Gloves

Pretty gloves for every day or a special occasion. Where I live, the month of July is the middle of winter, so I thought some brightly coloured gloves would add sunshine to a dreary time of year. They are begun in the round, then worked back and forth for the front opening, which is finished with small bobbles. Bobble edges are sewn together at intervals to create an openwork effect.

## SIZE
One size, to fit woman's small/medium hand. To make a larger size, use a slightly larger needle.

## FINISHED MEASUREMENTS
Hand circumference (approx): 16.5 cm (6½ in)

Length from tip of middle finger to cuff (approx): 25.5 cm (10 in)

## YARN
Koigu Premium Merino KPM [100% merino wool; 160 metres (175 yards) / 50 grams]: 2 hanks #1205 yellow or #2300 duck egg blue

## NEEDLES
Set of 2.75 mm double pointed

Set of 3 mm double pointed

Change needle size if necessary to obtain correct tension.

## NOTIONS
5 stitch markers (1 in a contrasting colour); tapestry needle; spare yarn

## TENSION
30 sts and 36 rnds = 10 cm (4 in) in St st using size 3 mm needles

*Special abbreviation: MB (make bobble): [K1, yo, k1] into next st, \*pass the 3 sts thus made back to left needle, k3; rep from \* once more, pass the 3 sts thus made back to left needle, slip 1, k2tog, psso.*

## LACE PATTERN
(multiple of 12 sts – 20 row rep)

**Row 1 and all WS rows:** Purl.
**Row 2:** K1, k2tog, k4, [yo, k1] twice, ssk, k1.
**Row 4:** K1, k2tog, k3, yo, k1, yo, k2, ssk, k1.
**Row 6:** K1, k2tog, k2, yo, k1, yo, k3, ssk, k1.
**Row 8:** K1, k2tog, [k1, yo] twice, k4, ssk, k1.
**Row 10:** K1, k2tog, yo, k1, yo, k5, ssk, k1.
**Row 12:** As Row 8.
**Row 14:** As Row 6.
**Row 16:** As Row 4.
**Row 18:** As Row 2.
**Row 20:** K1, k2tog, k5, yo, k1, yo, ssk, k1.
Rep Rows 1–20 for Lace Patt.

## LEFT GLOVE

With smaller dpns, cast on 45 sts, dividing evenly over 3 needles.
Join for working in the rnd, being careful not to twist sts; pcm for beg of rnd and sm on every rnd.
Work 10 rnds St st.
Purl 1 rnd (fold line).
Work 10 rnds St st.
Change to larger dpns and knit 2 rnds, inc 4 sts evenly across first rnd – 49 sts.\*\*
**Next rnd:** K28, pm, k12, pm, k1, cast off next 4 sts, knit to end, then k41 from beg of next rnd, turn – 45 sts.

Retaining contrast marker to indicate side seam and working back and forth in rows, commence Lace Patt as foll:

**Row 1 (WS):** P1, sm, work Row 1 of Lace Patt across next 12 sts, sm, purl to next marker, sm, p4.

Slipping markers on every row, cont working Lace Patt between markers as established, with St st either side, as foll: Work until completion of Row 11 of Lace Patt.

### Shape Thumb:

**Row 12:** Work 28, pm, m1r, k1, m1l, pm, work to end – 47 sts.
Work 2 rows even.

**Row 15:** Work 28, sm, m1pr, p3, m1pl, sm, work to end – 49 sts.
Work 2 rows even.

**Row 18:** Work 28, sm, m1r, k5, m1l, sm, work to end – 51 sts.
Cont as established, inc 1 st (as before) inside thumb markers on every foll 3rd row a further 5 times – 17 sts between thumb markers and 61 sts in all.

**Next row:** Work 28, remove marker, thread next 17 sts onto a piece of spare yarn, turn, cast on 1 st, turn, remove marker, work to end – 45 sts.

Work until completion of Row 20 of Lace Patt, then rep Rows 1–10 again, turn, cast on 4 sts, turn – 49 sts.

Join for working in the rnd and knit to side marker, removing markers for Lace Patt.

Knit 2 rnds.

### *** Little Finger:

**Rnd 1:** K6, place next 38 sts onto spare yarn, turn, cast on 1 st, turn, knit to side marker – 12 sts.

Working in rnds and slipping marker on every rnd, work until Little Finger measures 5.5 cm (2¼ in).

**Next rnd:** *K2tog; rep from * to end – 6 sts.

Break off yarn, thread onto tapestry needle, then draw yarn through each st. Pull up tightly and fasten off securely, then weave in end on WS.

Place 38 sts from spare yarn onto 3 mm dpns, dividing evenly over 3 needles; pu and knit 2 sts from cast-on st at base of Little Finger, placing a marker after first st; then knit to marker – 40 sts.

Knit 1 rnd.

### Ring Finger:

**Rnd 1:** K7, place next 26 sts onto spare yarn, turn, cast on 2 sts, turn, knit to marker – 16 sts.

Working in rnds and slipping marker on every rnd, work until
Ring Finger measures 7 cm (2¾ in).
Complete as for Little Finger.

### Middle Finger:
**Rnd 1:** Place first and last 6 sts of the 26 sts from spare yarn
onto dpns; pu and knit 2 sts from cast-on sts at base of Ring
Finger, placing a marker after first st; k6, turn, cast on 2 sts,
turn, then knit to marker – 16 sts.
Working in rnds and slipping marker on every rnd, work until
Middle Finger measures 7.5 cm (3 in).
Complete as for Little Finger.

### Index Finger:
**Rnd 1:** Place rem 14 sts from spare yarn onto dpns, pu and
knit 2 sts from cast-on sts at base of Middle Finger, placing a
marker after first of these 2 sts, then knit to marker – 16 sts.
Working in rnds and slipping marker on every rnd, work until
Index Finger measures 7 cm (2¾ in).
Complete as for Little Finger.

### Thumb:
Place 17 sts from spare yarn onto larger dpns, dividing evenly
over 3 needles, pu and knit 1 st into the cast-on st of hand
and join for working in the rnd – 18 sts.
Work in rnds until Thumb measures 5.5 cm (2¼ in).
Complete as for Little Finger. ***

## FINISHING

Using tapestry needle, weave in ends on WS using yarn at
base of fingers and thumb to close any holes.

### Left Front Opening Edging:
With RS facing and two smaller dpns, pu and knit 37 sts evenly
along left front opening edge.
Knit 1 row.
**Cast-off row:** *MB, cast off knitwise st just worked and foll 5
sts, pass st on right needle back to left needle; rep from * to
last st, MB.
Fasten off.

### Right Front Opening Edging:
Work as for Left Front Opening Edging.
Turn glove inside out. Sew sides of Front Opening Edgings to
cast-off and cast-on 4 sts of hand.

Sew Front Opening Edgings together at bobbles only, leaving openings in between.

Turn cast-on edge of glove to WS along fold line and stitch in place.

## RIGHT GLOVE

Work as for Left Glove to **.

**Next rnd:** K4, cast off next 4 sts, k1, pm, k12, pm, knit to marker, then k4 from beg of next rnd, turn – 45 sts.

Retaining contrast marker to indicate side seam and working back and forth in rows, commence Lace Patt as foll:

**Row 1 (WS):** P4, sm, purl to next marker, sm, work Row 1 of Lace Patt across next 12 sts, sm, p1.

Slipping markers on every row, cont working Lace Patt between markers as established, with St st either side, as foll: Work until completion of Row 11 of Lace Patt.

**Shape Thumb:**

**Row 12:** Work 16, pm, m1r, k1, m1l, pm, work to end – 47 sts.

Work 2 rows even.

**Row 15:** Work 16, sm, m1pr, p3, m1pl, sm, work to end – 49 sts.

Work 2 rows even.

**Row 18:** Work 16, sm, m1r, k5, m1l, sm, work to end – 51 sts.

Cont as established, inc 1 st (as before) inside thumb markers in every foll 3rd row a further 5 times – 17 sts between thumb markers and 61 sts in all.

**Next row:** Work 16, remove marker, thread next 17 sts onto a piece of spare yarn, turn, cast on 1 st, turn, remove marker, work to end – 45 sts.

Work until completion of Row 20 of Lace Patt, then rep Rows 1–10 again, turn, cast on 4 sts, turn – 49 sts.

Join for working in the rnd and knit to side marker, removing markers for Lace Patt.

Knit 2 rnds.

Complete as for Left Glove from *** to ***.

## FINISHING

Work as for Left Glove.

# Lulu Scarf

I experimented with geometric shapes to make this scarf. Trapezoids and triangles knitted in garter stitch create an undulating shape with one straight and one asymmetrical edge. It can be worn as a scarf, or draped delicately around the shoulders to form a little shawl. Even if you're a strict minimalist and do not indulge in ruffles as a rule, a soft feminine scarf like this is dramatic and flattering. The soft kid mohair and silk blend makes it light and feathery.

## FINISHED MEASUREMENTS
Length (approx): 140 cm (55 in)

Width at widest point (approx): 24 cm (9½ in)

## YARN
Rowan Kidsilk Haze [70% super kid mohair / 30% silk; 209 metres (229 yards) / 25 grams]: 3 balls #423 heavenly

## NEEDLES
3.5 mm x 80 cm (32 in) circular

Change needle size if necessary to obtain correct tension.

## NOTIONS
8 stitch markers; tapestry needle

## TENSION
24 sts and 40 rows = 10 cm (4 in) in garter stitch using size 3.5 mm (US 4) needle

## SCARF

Cast on 233 sts using cable cast-on method (see page 126). Work back and forth in rows as foll:

**\*\* Foundation row (WS):** P1, \*pm, k57, pm, p1; rep from \* to end.

**Row 1 (RS):** Slip 1 purlwise wyib, \*sm, ssk, knit to 2 sts before marker, k2tog, sm, slip 1 purlwise wyib; rep from \* to end – 225 sts.

**Row 2:** P1, \*sm, knit to marker, sm, p1; rep from \* to end.

Rep Rows 1 & 2 until 33 sts rem (7 sts between markers), ending with Row 1 and removing markers on last row. Do not turn.

Pu and knit 25 sts evenly along edge of last triangle, turn, cast on 175 sts using cable cast-on method – 233 sts.

Rep from \*\* 3 times more.

Rep Foundation row, then rep Rows 1 & 2 until 33 sts rem (7 sts between markers), ending with Row 1 and removing markers on last row. Do not turn.

Pu and knit 26 sts evenly along edge of last triangle, turn – 59 sts.

**Row 1 (WS):** P1, k57, p1.

**Row 2:** Slip 1 purlwise wyib, ssk, knit to last 3 sts, k2tog, slip 1 purlwise wyib – 57 sts.

Rep Rows 1 & 2 until 5 sts rem, ending with Row 1.

**Next row:** Slip 1 purlwise wyib, sk2p, slip 1 purlwise wyib – 3 sts.

**Next row:** P1, k1, p1.

**Next row:** Sk2p.

Fasten off.

Using tapestry needle, weave in ends on WS.

# Mrs Lovechild Shawl

I named this shawl after Ellenor Fenn, a children's author who wrote under the pen names Mrs Lovechild and Mrs Teachwell. She lived in the 18th century but her ideas were decidedly modern. The body of the shawl is worked from the top down, the lace edging knitted lengthways and sewn around the bottom edge. Stitches are picked up around the neck edge for the collar. Because the yarn used contains some angora, it is thicker than a normal lace-weight yarn and knits more like a light fingering or sock yarn.

## FINISHED MEASUREMENTS

Width across back at lower edge: 50 (55.5:61.5) cm [19¾ (21¾: 24¼) in]

Length from neck to lower edge, including edging (approx): 27 (29.5:32) cm [10½ (11½:12½) in]

## YARN

Naturally Lace [60% merino / 40% dehaired angora; 227 metres (248 yards) / 25 grams]: 5 balls #2

*Note: The shawl is worked with two strands of yarn held together.*

## NEEDLES

Pair 3.5 mm straight

Pair 4 mm straight

3.5 mm x 80 cm (32 in) circular

4 mm x 80 cm (32 in) circular

Change needle size if necessary to obtain correct tension.

## NOTIONS

2 stitch markers; 2 stitch holders; tapestry needle

## TENSION

21.5 sts and 32 rows = 10 cm (4 in) in St st using size 4 mm needles (US 6) and 2 strands of yarn

23 sts and 28 rows = 10 cm (4 in) in Lace Edge Pattern using size 4 mm needles and 2 strands of yarn

## LACE EDGE PATTERN

(Worked over 13 sts – 14 row rep)

**Row 1 and all WS rows:** K2, purl to last 2 sts, k2.

**Row 2:** Slip 1 knitwise, k3, yo, k5, yo, k2tog, yo, k2 – 15 sts.

**Row 4:** Slip 1 knitwise, k4, sk2p, k2, [yo, k2tog] twice, k1 – 13 sts.

**Row 6:** Slip 1 knitwise, k3, skp, k2, [yo, k2tog] twice, k1 – 12 sts.

**Row 8:** Slip 1 knitwise, k2, skp, k2, [yo, k2tog] twice, k1 – 11 sts.

**Row 10:** Slip 1 knitwise, k1, skp, k2, [yo, k2tog] twice, k1 – 10 sts.

**Row 12:** K1, skp, k2, yo, k1, yo, k2tog, yo, k2 – 11 sts.

**Row 14:** Slip 1 knitwise, [k3, yo] twice, k2tog, yo, k2 – 13 sts.

Rep Rows 1–14 for Lace Edge Pattern.

## SHAWL

With larger circular needle and 2 strands of yarn, cast on 48 (52:56) sts.

Work back and forth in rows as foll:

**Row 1 (WS):** K4, pm, k40 (44:48), pm, k4.

**Row 2:** *K1, yo, knit to 1 st before marker, yo, k1, sm; rep from * once more, k1, yo, knit to last st, yo, k1 – 54 (58:62) sts.

**Row 3:** K1, p1, pfb, purl to last 4 sts, pfb, p2, k1 – 56 (60:64) sts.

Rep Rows 2 & 3 a further 32 (36:40) times, then Row 2 once – 318 (354:390) sts.

**Next row (WS):** Knit.

Cast off loosely knitwise.

## EDGING

### Right Front:

Commence mitred point:

With larger straight needles and 2 strands of yarn, cast on 3 sts.

**Row 1 (RS):** K1, yo, k2 – 4 sts.

**Row 2:** K2, pfb, k1 – 5 sts.

**Row 3:** K1, yo, knit to end – 6 sts.

**Row 4:** K2, p1, pfb, k2 – 7 sts.

**Row 5:** K1, yo, knit to end – 8 sts.

**Row 6:** K2, purl to last 3 sts, pfb, k2 – 9 sts.

Rep Rows 5 & 6 twice more – 13 sts.

### Commence Pattern:

*Work Rows 2–14 of Lace Edge Patt once, then Rows 1–14 a further 8 (9:10) times.

### Corner Shaping:

**Row 1:** K2, p9, wrap, turn.

**Row 2:** K2, yo, k5, yo, k2tog, yo, k2.

**Row 3:** K2, p9, wrap, turn.

**Row 4:** K1, sk2p, k2, [yo, k2tog] twice, k1.

**Row 5:** K2, p7, purl wrap tog with the wrapped st, turn.

**Row 6:** K1, skp, k2, [yo, k2tog] twice, k1.

**Row 7:** K2, p8, purl wrap tog with the wrapped st, turn.

**Row 8:** K2, skp, k2, [yo, k2tog] twice, k1.

Work Rows 9–14 of Lace Edge Patt once.

### Back:

Work Rows 1–14 of Lace Edge Patt 10 (11:12) times.

Work Corner Shaping as before.

### Left Front:

Work Rows 1–14 of Lace Edge Patt 9 (10:11) times.

Commence mitred point:

**Row 1 (WS):** K2, purl to last 2 sts, k2.

**Row 2:** K1, yo, sk2p, knit to end – 12 sts.

**Row 3:** K2, purl to last 4 sts, p2tog, p1, k1 – 11 sts.

Rep Rows 2 & 3 a further 3 times – 5 sts.

**Row 10:** K1, sk2p, k1 – 3 sts.

Cast off purlwise.

Block lace strip lightly and sew in place evenly along lower edge of shawl, easing around corners.

## SHAWL COLLAR

With RS facing, smaller circular needle, 2 strands of yarn and beg at lower edge of Right Front, pu and knit 14 sts evenly along lace section, 63 (70:77) sts evenly along right front neck, 40 (44:48) sts evenly across back neck, 63 (70:77) sts evenly along left front neck to lace section, then 14 sts evenly along lace section – 194 (212:230) sts.

Work back and forth in rows as foll:

**Row 1 (WS):** Knit.

**Row 2:** K3, kfb, knit to last 5 sts, kfb, k4 – 196 (214:232) sts.

Rep Rows 1 & 2 a further 5 times – 206 (224:242) sts.

Knit 3 rows even.

**Next row:** K3, kfb, knit to last 5 sts, kfb, k4 – 208 (226:244) sts.

Knit 3 rows even.

**Next row:** K3, kfb, knit to last 5 sts, kfb, k4 – 210 (228:246) sts.

Knit 1 row even.

**Next row (RS):** Cast off 42 (47:52) sts loosely, knit to last 42 (47:52) sts, cast off next 42 (47:52) sts loosely – 126 (134:142) sts.

Break off yarn.

With WS facing, rejoin 2 strands of yarn to rem sts and knit 4 rows even.

## Shape Collar:

**Row 1:** K3, ssk, knit to last 5 sts, k2tog, k3 – 124 (132:140) sts.

Cont in garter st throughout, dec 1 st (as before) inside 3 sts each end of every foll 4th row 10 times – 104 (112:120) sts.

Dec 1 st (as before) inside 3 sts each end of next 9 rows – 86 (94:102) sts.

## Collar Edgings:

**Next row (WS):** K3, place these 3 sts onto a stitch holder; ssk, k1 and cast off previous st, cast off st just worked and all foll sts to last 5 sts, k2tog and cast off previous st, cast off st just worked, k2 – 3 sts. Change to smaller straight needles.

Cont on rem 3 sts until piece reaches halfway across cast-off edge of Collar. Place sts onto a stitch holder.

With RS facing, smaller straight needles and 2 strands of yarn, k3 from first stitch holder. Work until piece reaches halfway across cast-off edge of Collar.

Break off yarn, leaving a 20 cm (8 in) tail and thread onto tapestry needle. Graft sts of Collar Edgings together using Kitchener Stitch (see page 126).

## FINISHING

Using tapestry needle and placing seam of Collar Edgings to centre back of Collar, sew evenly to straight edge on RS.

Weave in ends on WS.

# Shiraz Slippers

This is a quick and easy project. I added suede pads to the soles so that they would last longer, but they are perfectly comfortable without. If they stretch after a while, you can machine wash them, even with the suede pads, and they will shrink back to a snug fit again. The finished lengths are long to accommodate the pointed toe, which rounds out slightly when worn.

## SIZES

Women's small (medium:large)

To fit foot length:
18–20 (20–23: 23–25.5) cm
[7–8 (8–9: 9–10) in]

## FINISHED MEASUREMENTS

Before felting:
Length: 31 (33:35) cm
[12 1/4 (13:13 3/4) in]

Width of sole at widest point:
9 cm (3 1/2 in)

After felting:
Length (approx):
25.5 (27.5:28.5) cm
[10 (10 3/4:11 1/4) in]

Width of sole at widest point
(approx): 7.5 cm (3 in)

## YARN

Cascade 220 [100% merino
wool; 201 metres (220 yards) /
100 grams]: 1 hank #2440 vinci
heather (A)

*NOTE: Slippers are worked using
2 strands of yarn held together.*

## NEEDLES

9 mm x 40 cm (16 in) circular

Pair 9 mm straight for Kitchener
Stitch

Change needle size if necessary
to obtain correct tension.

## NOTIONS

3 stitch markers (1 in a contrasting
colour); tapestry needle; spare
yarn for casting on; 20 cm (8 in)
ribbon 1 cm (1/2 in) wide for heel
trim (optional); sewing needle and
thread (optional)

For soles (optional): 20 x 30 cm
(8 x 11 3/4 in) piece soft suede; hole
puncher

## TENSION

9 sts and 14 rnds = 10 cm (4 in) in
St st using size 9 mm needles and
2 strands of yarn

## SLIPPER (Make 2)

(Commence at sole)

With circular needle and spare yarn, cast on 44 (48:52) sts.
With 2 strands of A, purl 1 row, leaving a 1 metre (3 foot) tail.
Join for working in the rnd, being careful not to twist sts; pcm
for beg of rnd and sm on every rnd.

**Rnd 1:** K22 (24:26), pm, m1, pm, knit to end – 45 (49:53) sts.
**Rnd 2:** Purl to marker, sm, m1p, p1, m1p, sm, purl to end –
47 (51:55) sts.
**Rnd 3:** K1, m1, *k2, m1, k1, m1, k15 (17:19), m1, k1, m1, k2; *sm, k1,
[m1, k1] twice, sm, rep from * to * once, m1, k1 – 59 (63:67) sts.
**Rnd 4:** Purl to marker, sm, p2, m1p, p1, m1p, p2, sm, purl to
end – 61 (65:69) sts.
**Rnd 5:** Knit to marker, sm, k3, m1, k1, m1, k3, sm, knit to end –
63 (67:71) sts.
**Rnd 6:** Purl to marker, sm, p4, m1p, p1, m1p, p4, sm, purl to
end – 65 (69:73) sts.

### Commence Turning:

Work back and forth in rows as foll:

**Row 1 (RS):** Knit to marker, sm, k5, m1, k1, m1, k5, sm,
k10 (12:14), wrap, turn – 67 (71:75) sts.
**Row 2:** Knit to marker, sm, k13, sm, k10 (12:14), wrap, turn.
**Row 3:** Knit to marker, sm, k6, m1, k1, m1, k6, sm, k8 (10:12),
wrap, turn – 69 (73:77) sts.
**Row 4:** Knit to marker, sm, k15, sm, k8 (10:12), wrap, turn.
**Row 5:** Knit to marker, sm, k7, m1, k1, m1, k7, sm, knit to end,
do not turn – 71 (75:79) sts.

### Slipper Upper:

**Row 1 (RS):** Knit to marker, sm, k6, ssk, k1, k2tog, k6, sm,
k4 (6:8), wrap, turn – 69 (73:77) sts.
**Row 2:** Purl to marker, sm, p5, p2tog, p1, p2tog tbl, p5, sm,
p4 (6:8), wrap, turn – 67 (71:75) sts.
**Row 3:** Knit to marker, sm, k4, ssk, k1, k2tog, k4, sm, knit to
end, do not turn – 65 (69:73) sts.

Commence working in rnds as foll:

**Rnd 1:** Knit to marker, sm, k3, ssk, k1, k2tog, k3, sm, knit to
end – 63 (67:71) sts.
**Rnd 2:** Knit to marker, sm, k2, ssk, k1, k2tog, k2, sm, knit to
end – 61 (65:69) sts.
**Rnd 3:** Knit to marker, sm, k1, ssk, k1, k2tog, k1, sm, knit to end –
59 (63:67) sts.

**Rnd 4:** Knit to marker, sm, ssk, k1, k2tog, sm, knit to end – 57 (61:65) sts.

**Rnd 5:** K1, k2tog, k6, k2tog, k6 (8:10), k2tog, k7, ssk (removing marker), k1, k2tog (removing marker), k7, ssk, k6 (8:10), ssk, k6, ssk, k1 – 49 (53:57) sts.

**Rnd 6:** K22 (24:26), ssk, k1, k2tog, knit to end – 47 (51:55) sts.

**Rnd 7:** Cast off purlwise 16 (18:20) sts; cast off knitwise 13 sts while working as foll: k4 (excluding st already on right-hand needle after cast-off), ssk, k1, k2tog, k4; cast off purlwise to end.

## FINISHING

Turn slipper inside out.

Remove spare yarn from cast-on sts whilst placing 22 (24:26) sts on each of two size 13 straight needles, with points facing towards heel. Thread tapestry needle with yarn tail at heel, then graft sts from both needles together on WS using Kitchener Stitch (see page 126).

Weave in ends on WS.

Felt to size (see page 126). If slippers stretch after they've been worn for a while, you can felt them again to pull them back into shape.

## SOLES (optional)

*See photograph on the back cover.*

Cut two 5 x 9 cm (2 x 3½ in) ovals of suede and a further two 8 x 12 cm (3 x 4¾ in) ovals of suede (see actual size template opposite). On WS of suede pieces, draw dots 5 mm (¼ in) apart and 5 mm (¼ in) in from edges. Punch holes to correspond with dots. Once slippers are dry after felting, pin pieces in place on sole of slippers and sew in place using blanket stitch.

If desired, use sewing needle and thread to sew ribbon in place up centre back of heel, turning over and making a loop 1 cm (½ in) deep at the ankle.

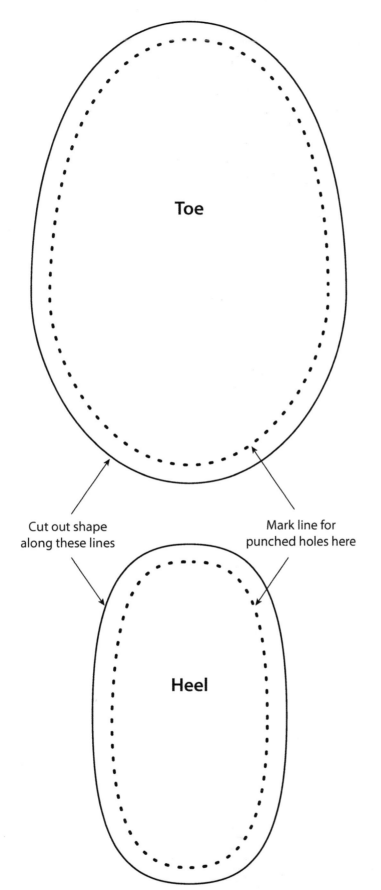

**SHIRAZ SLIPPERS SOLE TEMPLATE**

Use this actual size template to mark and cut out suede pieces to sew onto the botto of your slippers (see pattern page 78).

Toe

Cut out shape along these lines

Mark line for punched holes here

Heel

# Marilyn Shorts

These shorts could be worn as pyjamas or streetwear, perhaps over tights. They are secured by elastic around the hips. The ribbon tie is optional.

## SIZES
To fit waist: 61–66 (71–76:81–86: 92–97:102–107) cm [24–26 (28–30:32–34:36–38:40–42) in]

## FINISHED MEASUREMENTS
Waist (approx):
80 (90.5:101.5:110:121) cm [31½(35½:40: 43¼:47½) in]

Length: 28 (30.5:30.5:33:33) cm [11 (12:12:13:13) in]

## YARN
Rowan Wool Cotton [50% merino wool / 50% cotton; 113 metres (123 yards) / 50 grams]: 4 (4:4:5:5) balls #968 cypress (A) and 1 ball #941 clear (B)

## NEEDLES
3.25 mm x 80 cm (32 in) circular

3.5 mm x 80 cm (32 in) circular

Change needle size if necessary to obtain correct tension.

## NOTIONS
Stitch holder; stitch marker; tapestry needle; 1.5 cm (⅝ in) wide elastic to fit comfortably around waist; sewing needle and thread; 1 metre (1 yard) ribbon 1 cm (⅜ in) wide (optional)

## TENSION
21.5 sts and 30 rows = 10 cm (4 in) in St st using size 3.5 mm needle

## STRIPE PATTERN

2 rows B in St st.
2 rows A in St st.

## LEFT LEG

With smaller needle and A, cast on 120 (132:146:158:170) sts. Work back and forth in rows as foll:

Work 7 rows St st, beg with a knit row.

Knit 1 row (fold line).

Work 6 rows St st, beg with a knit row.

Change to larger needle and B.

*NOTE: Do not break off yarn after each stripe; instead, carry up side of work.*

Work 14 rows stripe pattern, thus ending with 2 rows B.

### Shape Crotch:
Cont in stripe pattern, dec 1 st at each end of next row, then on every foll alt row 4 times, then on every foll 4th row twice – 106 (118:132:144:156) sts.

Break off B and cont in A only.

Dec 1 st at each end of every foll 4th row until 90 (106:118:130:142) sts rem.

### *Larger Four Sizes Only:*
Dec 1 st at each end of every foll 6th row until 102 (114:124:136) sts rem.

### *All Sizes:*
Work straight until leg measures 25.5 (28:28:30.5:30.5) cm [10 (11:11:12:12) in] from fold line, ending with a WS row.

### Shape Back:
**Row 1:** Work 44 (50:56:61:67), wrap, turn.
**Row 2:** Work to end.
**Row 3:** Work 42 (48:54:59:65), wrap, turn.

**Row 4:** Work to end.
**Row 5:** Work 40 (46:52:57:63), wrap, turn.
**Row 6:** Work to end.
**Row 7:** Work 38 (44:50:55:61), wrap, turn.
**Row 8:** Work to end. **
Place sts onto a stitch holder.

### RIGHT LEG

Work as for Left Leg to **, working 1 row less before shaping back.
**Next row:** Purl to end across all sts.

### Join Legs:

With RS facing, knit across sts of Right Leg, then knit across sts of Left Leg, thus ending at centre front – 180 (204:228:248:272) sts.
Join for working in the rnd, pm for beg of rnd and sm on every rnd.
Knit 1 rnd.
Change to smaller circular needle.
Knit 1 rnd (knit 1 more rnd here if not working eyelet rnd).
**Eyelet rnd (optional):** K4, yo, k2tog, knit to last 5 sts, yo, k2tog, k3.
Knit 4 rnds.
Purl 1 rnd (fold line).
Knit 7 rnds.
Cast off.

### FINISHING

Using tapestry needle, weave in ends on WS.
Sew each leg seam to beg of crotch shaping, then sew front and back seams.
Fold leg hems to inside along fold line and sew in place on WS.
Fold waistband to inside along fold line and sew loosely in place on WS, leaving an opening at centre front to insert elastic.
Cut a length of elastic slightly smaller than waist measurement. Thread elastic through waistband and use sewing needle and thread to sew ends together.
Cut 2 lengths of ribbon (optional) and use sewing needle and thread to sew to elastic to correspond with eyelets. Thread ribbon through eyelets and tie in a bow.
Sew opening closed at centre front.

# Everyday Cardigan

Even if you're shy about showing your waist, there's no need to be afraid of a cropped cardigan. I wear mine over a long shirt or a dress so that my secrets are hidden while the cardigan gives me shape. It's knit in one piece to the armholes, with elongated cuffs and a placket in twisted rib stitch. The buttonhole is large enough to accommodate a chunky vintage button.

## SIZES
To fit bust: 81 (86:92:97:102:107: 112:117) cm [32 (33¾:36¼:38¼: 40¼:42¼:44:46) in]

## FINISHED MEASUREMENTS
Bust circumference:
86 (92:97:102:107:112:117:122) cm [33¾ (36¼:38¼:40¼:42¼:44: 46:48) in]

Length to shoulder:
41 (41:42:42: 43:43:44:44) cm [16¼ (16¼:16½:16½:17:17:17¼: 17¼) in]

Sleeve length: 46 cm (18 in)

## YARN
Cascade 220 [100% merino wool; 201 metres (220 yards) / 100 grams]: 4 (4:5:5:5:5:5:6) hanks #2441 river rock heather

## NEEDLES
Pair 4 mm straight

4 mm x 80 cm (32 in) circular

Extra 4 mm straight, for three-needle cast-off (optional)

Change needle size if necessary to obtain correct tension.

## NOTIONS
2 stitch markers; tapestry needle; 4 stitch holders; 3 cm (1¼ in) button

## TENSION
22 sts and 26 rows = 10 cm (4 in) in St st using size 4 mm needles

## TWISTED RIB STITCH
**Special abbreviation:** *T2P (twist 2 purlways) = Purl into front of second st on left-hand needle, then purl first st, slipping both off needle together.*
(multiple of 3+1 sts)
**Row 1 (RS):** *P1, k2; rep from * to last st, p1.
**Row 2:** *K1, T2P; rep from * to last st, k1.
Rep Rows 1 & 2.

## BACK AND FRONTS
With circular needle, cast on 31 (34:36:38:40:43:45:48) sts, pm, cast on a further 91 (97:103:107:113:119:123:129) sts, pm, cast on a further 31 (34:36:38:40:43:45:48) sts – 153 (165:175: 183:193:205:213:225) sts.
Work back and forth in rows, slipping markers on every row to indicate side seams and working in St st as foll:
**Row 1 (WS):** Purl.

### Shape Fronts:
Inc 1 st at each end of next row, then on every foll alt row 2 (2:4:4:6:6:6:6) times, then on every foll 4th row 2 (2:1:1: 0:0:0:0) time(s) – 163 (175:187:195:207:219:227:239) sts. Work 3 rows.

### Shape Sides:
**Inc row (RS):** Inc 1 st at beg of row, *knit to 1 st before marker, kfb, sm, kfb; rep from * once, knit to end, inc 1 st at end of row – 169 (181:193:201:213:225:233:245) sts.
Inc 1 st at each end of every foll 4th row twice – 173 (185:197: 205:217:229:237:249) sts.
Work straight until piece measures 14 cm (5¾ in) from beg, ending with a WS row.

## Shape Front Slopes:
Dec 1 st at each end of next row, then on foll alt row –
169 (181:193:201:213:225:233:245) sts.
Work 1 row.

## RIGHT FRONT

Change to straight needles.
**Next row (RS):** Dec 1 st at beg of row, knit to marker, turn and
cont on these 37 (40:43:45:48:51:53:56) sts only for Right Front,
leaving rem sts on circular needle to work later.

### Shape Armhole:
**Next row (WS):** Cast off 4 (4:5:5:6:7:8:9) sts, purl to end –
33 (36: 38:40:42:44:45:47) sts.
** Dec 1 st at armhole edge on next 3 (3:3:3:3:5:5:7) rows AT
SAME TIME dec 1 st at neck edge on next row, then on every foll
alt row 1 (1:1:1:1:2:2:3) time(s) – 28 (31:33:35:37:36:37:36) sts.
Dec 1 st at each end of every foll alt row 0 (1:1:1:2:2:2:2) time(s) –
28 (29:31:33:33:32:33:32) sts.
Keeping armhole edge straight, dec 1 st at neck edge on every
foll alt row until 22 (24:25:27:27:27:27:27) sts rem, then on
every foll 4th row until 15 (17:18:20:20:20:20:20) sts rem.
Work straight until piece measures 19 (19:20:20:21:21:22:22) cm
[7½ (7½:7¾:7¾:8¼:8¼:8⅝:8⅝) in] from beg of armhole
shaping, ending with a WS row.

### Shape Shoulder:
**Next row:** Work 10 (11:12:13:13:13:13:13), wrap, turn.
**Next row:** Work to end.
**Next row:** Work 5 (5:6:6:6:6:6:6), wrap, turn.
**Next row:** Work to end.
**Next row:** Work across all sts. **
Break off yarn and place sts onto a stitch holder for joining
shoulders.

## BACK

### Shape Armholes:
With RS facing and straight needles, join yarn to rem sts on
circular needle, cast off 4 (4:5:5:6:7:8:9) sts, knit to marker, turn
and cont on these 89 (95:100:104:109:114:117:122) sts only for
Back, leaving rem sts on circular needle to work later.
**Next row:** Cast off 4 (4:5:5:6:7:8:9) sts, purl to end –
85 (91:95:99:103:107:109:113) sts.
Dec 1 st at each end of next 3 (3:3:3:3:5:5:7) rows, then on
every foll alt row 0 (1:1:1:2:2:2:2) time(s) –

79 (83:87: 91:93:93:95:95) sts.

Work straight until piece measures 19 (19:20:20:21:21:22:22) cm [7½ (7½:7¾:7¾:8¼:8¼:8⅝:8⅝) in] from beg of armhole shaping, ending with a WS row.

### Shape Back Neck and Shoulders:

**Next row:** K17 (19:20:22:22:22:22:22), turn and cont on these sts only.

**Next row:** Cast off 1 st, purl to last 5 (6:6:7:7:7:7:7) sts, wrap, turn.

**Next row:** Knit to last 2 sts, k2tog.

**Next row:** P5 (5:6:6:6:6:6:6), wrap, turn.

**Next row:** Knit to end.

**Next row:** Purl across all sts.

Break off yarn, leaving a length at least 4 times the width of shoulder sts for joining shoulders.

Place sts onto a stitch holder.

With RS facing, join yarn to rem Back sts, cast off 45 (45:47:47: 49:49:51:51) sts, knit to last 5 (6:6:7:7:7:7:7) sts, wrap, turn.

**Next row:** Purl to last 2 sts, p2tog.

**Next row:** Cast off 1 st, knit to last 10 (12:12:14:14:14:14:14) sts, wrap, turn.

**Next row:** Purl to end.

**Next row:** Knit across all sts.

Break off yarn and place sts onto a stitch holder for joining shoulders.

## LEFT FRONT

With RS facing and straight needles, join yarn to rem sts on circular needle for Left Front.

### Shape Armhole:

**Next row (RS):** Cast off 4 (4:5:5:6:7:8:9) sts, knit to end dec 1 st at end of row – 33 (36:38:40:42:44:45:47) sts.

Work 1 row.

Work as for Right Front from ** to **, working 1 row more before shoulder shaping.

Break off yarn, leaving a length at least 4 times the width of shoulder sts for joining shoulders.

Place sts onto a stitch holder.

## SLEEVES

With straight needles, cast on 58 (58:61:61:64:64:67:67) sts.

Work in Twisted Rib Stitch until piece measures 14 cm (5½ in) from beg, ending with Row 2.

# Patchwork Tote

Like the Lulu Scarf, this bag is an experiment with geometric shapes. Hexagons and pentagons are knitted separately and form a rounded bowl shape when sewn together before felting. You can make the bag in one colour for a sculptured effect, as seen in the photograph on page 8, or emphasize the patchwork by choosing several different colours.

## FINISHED MEASUREMENTS

Before felting:

Rim: 84 cm (33 in)

Depth: 52 cm (20 ½ in)

After felting:

Rim (approx): 71 cm (28 in)

Depth (approx): 38 cm (15 in)

## YARN

Manos Del Uruguay Wool Clasica [kettle-dyed pure wool; 126 metres (138 yards) / 100 grams]:
*Single-colour tote* – 4 hanks #72 pumpkin; *Multicolour tote* – 1 hank each #O rose (A), #24 blush (B), #K putty (C), #20 parma (D), #01 pink (E) and #71 wisteria (F)

## NEEDLES

Set of 9 mm double pointed

9 mm x 60 cm (24 in) circular

Change needle size if necessary to obtain correct tension.

## NOTIONS

1 stitch marker; 1 large Grayson E leather handle 60 cm (24 in) long; tapestry needle; sewing needle

## TENSION

10 sts and 14 rnds = 10 cm (4 in) in St st using size 9 mm needles

## SINGLE-COLOUR TOTE

Work as for Multicolour Tote, working in one shade throughout.

## MULTICOLOUR TOTE

### HEXAGON (Make 15 – 2 each in A, E & F; 3 each in B, C & D)

With dpns, cast on 12 sts evenly over 3 needles (4 sts on each needle).

Join for working in the rnd, being careful not to twist sts; pm for beg of rnd and sm on every rnd.

**Rnd 1:** Knit all sts tbl to end.

**Rnd 2:** *Kfb, k1; rep from * to end – 6 sts on each needle, 18 sts in all.

**Rnd 3:** Knit.

**Rnd 4:** *Kfb, k1, [kfb] into each of next 2 sts, k1, kfb; rep from * twice more – 30 sts.

**Rnds 5 & 6:** Knit.

**Rnd 7:** *Kfb, k3, [kfb] into each of next 2 sts, k3, kfb; rep from * twice more – 42 sts.

**Rnds 8 & 9:** Knit.

**Rnd 10:** *Kfb, k5, [kfb] into each of next 2 sts, k5, kfb; rep from * twice more – 54 sts.

**Rnd 11:** Knit.

Cast off loosely, leaving a 40 cm (16 in) tail.

With tapestry needle, close gap at centre of Hexagon and weave in end on WS.

Complete the outside edge by joining the first and last cast-off sts. Do not weave in end and set piece aside.

### PENTAGON (Make 11 – 1 each in D & F; 2 each in B, C & E; 3 in A)

With dpns, cast on 10 sts evenly over 3 needles.

Join for working in the rnd, being careful not to twist sts;

pm for beg of rnd and sm on every rnd.
**Rnd 1:** Knit all sts tbl to end.
**Rnd 2:** *K1, kfb; rep from * to end – 15 sts.
**Rnd 3:** Knit.
**Rnd 4:** [Kfb, k1, kfb] 5 times – 25 sts.
**Rnds 5 & 6:** Knit.
**Rnd 7:** [Kfb, k3, kfb] 5 times – 35 sts.
**Rnd 8:** Knit.
**Rnd 9:** [Kfb, k5, kfb] 5 times – 45 sts.
**Rnd 10:** Knit.
Cast off loosely, leaving a 40 cm (16 in) tail.
Complete as for Hexagon.

## FINISHING

Sew pieces together with whip stitch on RS, using yarn left at cast-off edge. Consult diagram for placement and beg with a pentagon surrounded by hexagons.
At the top opening of the bag there will be 5 part-hexagon spaces between the pentagons. In each of these spaces, work as foll:
With RS facing, circular needle and shade as indicated on diagram, pu and knit 7 sts along each of the 3 sides of one space – 21 sts.

Work in rows.
**Row 1 and all WS rows:** Purl.
**Row 2:** *K2tog, k3, ssk; rep from * twice more – 15 sts.
**Row 4:** *K2tog, k1, ssk; rep from * twice more – 9 sts.
**Row 6:** *K2tog, ssk, k1, ssk, k2tog – 5 sts.
Break off yarn, thread onto tapestry needle, then draw yarn through each st. Pull up tightly and fasten off securely.
Weave in end on WS.
Weave in any rem ends on WS.

**Edging:**
With RS facing, circular needle and B, pu and knit 15 sts across top of each part-hexagon – 75 sts.
Join for working in the rnd; pm for beg of rnd.
Purl 1 rnd, then knit 1 rnd.
Rep last 2 rnds once more.
Cast off loosely purlwise.
Felt to size (see page 126).
When bag is dry, using sewing needle and length of yarn, sew handle to WS of opening at each end of bag.

# CHART

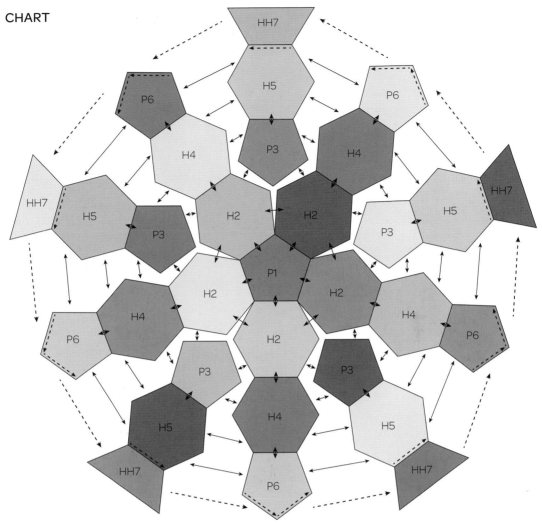

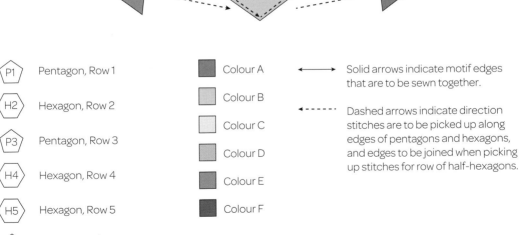

| | |
|---|---|
| (P1) | Pentagon, Row 1 |
| (H2) | Hexagon, Row 2 |
| (P3) | Pentagon, Row 3 |
| (H4) | Hexagon, Row 4 |
| (H5) | Hexagon, Row 5 |
| (P6) | Pentagon, Row 6 |
| (HH7) | Half-hexagon, Row 7 |

| | |
|---|---|
| ▮ | Colour A |
| ▮ | Colour B |
| ▮ | Colour C |
| ▮ | Colour D |
| ▮ | Colour E |
| ▮ | Colour F |

⟷ Solid arrows indicate motif edges that are to be sewn together.

⟵- - - Dashed arrows indicate direction stitches are to be picked up along edges of pentagons and hexagons, and edges to be joined when picking up stitches for row of half-hexagons.

# Everyday Vest

A cardigan vest is a wardrobe staple. It suits any style of dress and any man, young or old. I made this with a machine-washable wool and cotton blend. It's knit in one piece to the armholes.

## SIZES
To fit chest: 92–97 (102–107:
112–117:122–127:132–137) cm
[36–38 (40–42:44–46:48–50:
52–54) in]

## FINISHED MEASUREMENTS
Chest circumference:
101 (112:121:132:141) cm
[39 3/4 (44:47 3/4:52:55 1/4) in]

Length to shoulder:
70.5 (72:72.5:73.5:74) cm
[27 3/4 (28 1/4:28 1/2:29:29 1/4) in]

## YARN
Spud & Chloë Sweater Superwash
[55% wool / 45% organic cotton;
146 metres (160 yards) / 100 grams]:
5 (6:6:6:7) hanks #7506 toast

## NEEDLES
Pair 4 mm straight

4 mm x 80 cm (32 in) circular

4 mm x 40 cm (16 in) circular

Pair 4.5 mm straight

4.5 mm x 80 cm (32 in) circular

Extra 4.5 mm straight, for
three-needle cast-off

Change needle size if necessary
to obtain correct tension.

## NOTIONS
Six 2 cm (3/4 in) buttons; tapestry
needle; 3 stitch holders; stitch
marker; spare yarn

## TENSION
18 sts and 24 rows = 10 cm (4 in) in
St st using size 4.5 mm needles

## POCKET LININGS (Make 2)

With larger straight needles, cast on 21 (21:23:23:25) sts.
Work in St st, beg with a knit row, until piece measures 11 cm
(4 3/8 in), ending with a WS row.
Break off yarn and place sts onto a stitch holder.

## BACK AND FRONTS

(worked in one piece to armholes)
With smaller 80 cm circular needle, cast on
191 (211:227:247:261) sts.
Work back and forth in rows as foll:
**Row 1 (RS):** Slip 1 knitwise wyib, *p1, k1; rep from * to end.
**Row 2:** Slip 1 purlwise wyif, *k1, p1; rep from * to end.
Rep Rows 1 & 2 once more.
**Buttonhole row (RS):** Slip 1 knitwise wyib, *p1, k1; rep from *
to last 4 sts, yo, k2tog, p1, k1.
Rep Row 2 once more, then Rows 1 & 2 once.
**Next row:** Slip 1 knitwise wyib, [p1, k1] 3 times, place these
7 sts on spare yarn for Right Front Placket, knit to last 7 sts,
turn, place last 7 sts on spare yarn for Left Front Placket –
177 (197:213:233:247) sts.
Change to larger circular needle.
Work in St st, beg with a purl row, until piece measures 8.5 cm
(3 3/8 in) from beg of St st, ending with a WS row.

## Pocket Tops and Place Pocket:
**Row 1 (RS):** K11 (14:15:17:18), [p1, k1] 10 (10:11:11:12) times, p1,
knit to last 32 (35:38:40:43) sts, [p1, k1] 10 (10:11:11:12) times,
p1, knit to end.
**Row 2:** P11 (14:15:17:18), [k1, p1] 10 (10:11:11:12) times, k1, purl to last
32 (35:38:40:43) sts, [k1, p1] 10 (10:11:11:12) times, k1, purl to end.
Rep Rows 1 & 2 once more, then Row 1 once.
**Row 6:** P11 (14:15:17:18), cast off next 21 (21:23:23:25) sts
in rib, purl to last 32 (35:38:40:43) sts, cast off next
21 (21:23:23:25) sts in rib, purl to end.

**Row 7 (RS):** K11 (14:15:17:18), knit across sts of first Pocket Lining, knit to last 11 (14:15:17:18) sts, knit across sts of second Pocket Lining, knit to end – 177 (197:213:233:247) sts.
Work in St st, beg with a purl row, until piece measures 46 cm (18 in) or desired length from beg, ending with a WS row.

## RIGHT FRONT

Change to larger straight needles.
**Next row:** K43 (48:52:57:60), turn and cont on these sts only for Right Front, leaving rem sts on circular needle to work later.

### Shape Armhole:

**Next row (WS):** cast off 7 (8:9:10:10) sts, purl to end – 36 (40:43: 47:50) sts.
** Dec 1 st at armhole edge on next 3 (3:5:7:9) rows, then on every foll alt row 3 (3:2:1:0) time(s) – 30 (34:36:39:41) sts.
Purl 1 row.

### Shape Front Slope:

*Larger Four Sizes Only:*
Dec 1 st at each end of next row, then on every foll alt row 0 (1:3:5) time(s) – 32 (32:31:29) sts.
Purl 1 row.

*All Sizes:*
Keeping armhole edge straight, dec 1 st at neck edge on next row, then on every foll alt row until 20 (22:23:23:24) sts rem, then on every foll 4th row until 15 (17:17:17:17) sts rem.
Work straight until piece measures 23.5 (24.5:25.5:26.5:27.5) cm [9¼ (9½:10:10½:11) in] from beg of armhole shaping, ending with a WS row.

### Shape Shoulder:

**Next row:** Work 7 (8:8:8:8), wrap, turn.
**Next row:** Work to end.
**Next row:** Work across all sts. **
Break off yarn and place sts onto a stitch holder for joining shoulders.

## BACK

With RS facing and larger straight needles, join yarn to rem sts on circular needle, cast off 7 (8:9:10:10) sts, knit until there are 84 (93:100:109:117) sts on right needle, turn and cont on these sts only for Back, leaving rem sts on circular needle to work later.

**Next row:** Cast off 7 (8:9:10:10) sts, purl to end –
77 (85:91:99:107) sts.

Dec 1 st at each end of next 3 (3:5:7:9) rows, then on every foll
alt row 3 (4:4:5:6) times – 65 (71:73:75:77) sts.

Work straight until piece measures 23.5 (24.5:25.5:26.5:27.5) cm
[9¼ (9⅝:10:10⅜:10⅞) in] from beg of armhole shaping,
ending with a WS row.

### Shape Back Neck and Shoulders:

**Next row (RS):** K15 (17:17:17:17), turn and cont on these sts only.

**Next row:** P7 (8:8:8:8), wrap, turn.

**Next row:** Knit.

**Next row:** Purl across all sts.

Break off yarn, leaving a length at least 4 times the width of
shoulder sts for joining shoulders.

Place sts onto a stitch holder.

With RS facing, join yarn to rem Back sts, cast off
35 (37:39:41:43) sts, knit to last 8 (9:9:9:9) sts, wrap, turn.

**Next row:** Purl.

**Next row:** Knit across all sts.

Break off yarn and place sts onto a stitch holder for joining
shoulders.

## LEFT FRONT

With RS facing and larger straight needles, join yarn to rem sts
on circular needle for Left Front.

### Shape Armhole:

**Next row (RS):** Cast off 7 (8:9:10:10) sts, knit to end –
36 (40:43: 47:50) sts.

Purl 1 row.

Work as for Right Front from ** to **, working 1 row more
before shoulder shaping.

Do not break off yarn. Leave sts on needle.

## FINISHING

### Join Shoulders:

Place Left Back sts on larger straight needle so that points of
both Left Back and Left Front needles are facing same
direction.

With RS together and using an extra straight needle, join
shoulder using three-needle cast-off (see page 127).

Place Right Back and Right Front shoulder sts on two straight needles with points of both needles at same edge of work as length of yarn for joining shoulders.

With RS together and using an extra straight needle, join shoulder using three-needle cast-off.

### Right Front Placket:

With smaller straight needles, place Right Front Placket sts onto needle to beg with a WS row.

Join yarn and cont in rib (as before) until placket reaches (slightly stretched) up Right Front and across to centre of back neck (slightly stretched), ending with a WS row.

Break off yarn, leaving a length at least 4 times the width of placket.

Place sts onto a stitch holder.

Using tapestry needle, sew placket in place and mark button positions, the first to match buttonhole on Left Front, the top one to come just below beg of front slope shaping and the rem 4 spaced evenly between.

### Left Front Placket:

With smaller straight needles, place Left Front Placket sts onto needle to beg with a RS row.

Join yarn and cont in rib (as before) until placket reaches (slightly stretched) up Left Front and across to centre of back neck, ending with a WS row and working further buttonholes (as before) to correspond with markers on Right Front.

Do not break off yarn. Place sts onto a stitch holder.

Using tapestry needle, sew placket in place.

Join ends of plackets at centre of back neck using Kitchener Stitch for 1x1 Rib (page 127).

### Armhole Plackets (make 2):

With RS facing, 40 cm circular needle and beginning at underarm, pu and knit 102 (108:118:124:130) sts evenly around armhole edge.

Join for working in the rnd; pm for beg of rnd and sm on every rnd.

**Rnd 1:** *K1, p1; rep from * to end.

Rep Rnd 1 a further 4 times.

Cast off in rib.

Using tapestry needle, weave in ends on WS.

Sew pocket linings in place on WS. Sew buttons to right placket as marked.

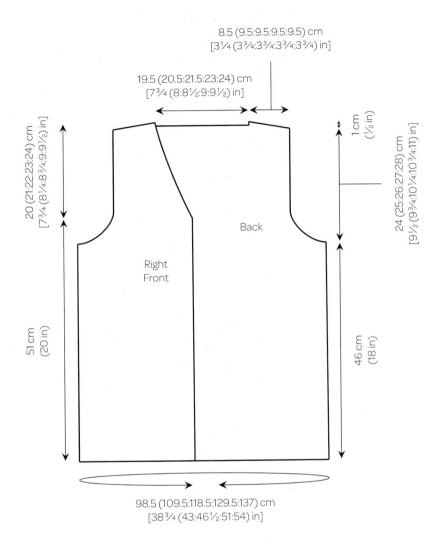

8.5 (9.5:9.5:9.5:9.5) cm
[3¼ (3¾:3¾:3¾:3¾) in]

19.5 (20.5:21.5:23:24) cm
[7¾ (8:8½:9:9½) in]

1 cm
(½ in)

20 (21:22:23:24) cm
[7¾ (8¼:8¾:9:9½) in]

24 (25:26:27:28) cm
[9½ (9¾:10¼:10¾:11) in]

Back

Right
Front

51 cm
(20 in)

46 cm
(18 in)

98.5 (109.5:118.5:129.5:137) cm
[38¾ (43:46½:51:54) in]

# Daisy Dachshund

I have loved making animals since I was a little girl. It's a delight to see their personalities emerge once they are completed, especially after the face is embroidered. In the midst of all the grown-up patterns in this book, I couldn't resist including a whimsical pencil case, which is named after a beloved family pet. It's an accessory to make a child feel special during a day at school. You can also make it as a soft toy.

## FINISHED MEASUREMENTS
Length from nose to base of tail:
30 cm (11 3/4 in)

## YARN
Cascade 220 [100% merino wool; 201 metres (220 yards) / 100 grams]: 1 hank #2435 Japanese maple heather

## NEEDLES
Pair 4.5 mm straight

Extra 4.5 mm straight, for three-needle cast -off

Change needle size if necessary to obtain correct tension.

## NOTIONS
4 stitch holders; tapestry needle; fibre filling; small amount of black yarn for embroidery of nose and eyes

For pencil case only: 22 x 20 cm (8 1/2 x 8 in) piece of lining fabric; small pieces of fabric for lining tops of legs and head opening; 20 x 30 cm (8 x 12 in) piece of iron-on interfacing; sewing needle and thread; 18 cm (7 in) zip

## TENSION
21 sts and 28 rows = 10 cm (4 in) in St st using size 4.5 mm needles

## FRONT LEGS (Make 2)

Cast on 15 sts.
**Row 1 (RS):** Knit.
**Row 2:** Purl.
**Row 3:** K6, sk2p, k6 – 13 sts.
Work 5 rows St st, beg with a purl row.
Break off yarn and place sts onto a stitch holder.

## LEFT BACK LEG

Cast on 15 sts.
**Row 1 (RS):** Knit.
**Row 2:** Purl.
**Row 3:** K6, sk2p, k6 – 13 sts.
Work 3 rows St st, beg with a purl row.
**Row 7:** Skp, knit to last 2 sts, k2tog – 11 sts.
**Row 8:** Purl. **
**Row 9:** Knit.
**Row 10:** Cast off 6 sts purlwise, purl to end – 5 sts.
Break off yarn and place sts onto a stitch holder.

## RIGHT BACK LEG

Work as for Left Back Leg to **.
**Row 9:** Cast off 6 sts, knit to end – 5 sts.
**Row 10:** Purl.
Break off yarn and place sts onto a stitch holder.

## LEFT SIDE BODY

With RS facing, work across sts of Left Back Leg as foll: k4, m1, k1, turn, cast on 23 sts, turn, work across sts of Left Front Leg as foll: k5, m1, knit to end – 43 sts.

**Row 1 (WS):** Cast off 7 sts purlwise, purl to end – 36 sts.
**Row 2:** Kfb, knit to last 2 sts, kfb, k1 – 38 sts.
**Row 3:** Pfb, purl to end – 39 sts.
Rep Rows 2 & 3 a further 4 times – 51 sts.

Shape Head:
**Row 1 (RS):** Kfb, knit to last 2 sts, kfb, k1, turn, cast on 8 sts – 61 sts.
**Row 2:** Purl.
**Row 3:** Knit to last 2 sts, kfb, k1 – 62 sts.
**Rows 4 & 5:** Rep Rows 2 & 3 once – 63 sts.
**Row 6:** P3, wrap, turn.
**Row 7:** K3.
**Row 8:** Spp, purl to end – 62 sts.
Rep Rows 7 & 8 once more – 61 sts.

Shape Tail:
**Row 1 (RS):** Cast on 18 sts by Cable Cast-on method (see page 126), cast off 9 sts (from those just cast on), knit to end – 70 sts.
**Row 2:** Spp, purl to end – 69 sts.
**Row 3:** Cast off 10 sts, knit to last 2 sts, k2tog – 58 sts.
**Row 4:** Purl.
**Row 5:** Cast off 43 sts, knit to last 2 sts, k2tog – 14 sts.
**Row 6:** Purl.
**Row 7:** Skp, knit to last 2 sts, k2tog – 12 sts.

**Rows 8 & 9:** Rep Rows 6 & 7 once – 10 sts.
**Row 10:** Spp, purl to last 2 sts, p2tog – 8 sts.
**Row 11:** Skp, knit to last 2 sts, k2tog – 6 sts.
Cast off purlwise.

## RIGHT SIDE BODY

With RS facing, work across sts of Right Front Leg as foll: cast off 7 sts (1 st on right needle), m1, k5, turn, cast on 23 sts, turn, work across sts of Right Back Leg as foll: k1, m1, k4 – 36 sts.
**Row 1 (WS):** Purl.
**Row 2:** Kfb, knit to last 2 sts, kfb, k1 – 38 sts.
**Row 3:** Purl to last 2 sts, pfb, p1 – 39 sts.
Rep Rows 2 & 3 a further 4 times – 51 sts.

### Shape Head:

**Row 1 (RS):** Cast on 8 sts by Cable Cast-on method, k8, kfb, knit to last 2 sts, kfb, k1 – 61 sts.
**Row 2:** Purl.
**Row 3:** Kfb, knit to end – 62 sts.
**Row 4:** Purl.
**Row 5:** Kfb, k1, wrap, turn – 63 sts.
**Row 6:** P3.
**Row 7:** Skp, knit to end – 62 sts.
Rep Rows 6 & 7 once more – 61 sts.

### Shape Tail:

**Row 1 (WS):** Cast on 18 sts purlwise by Cable Cast-on method, Cast off 9 sts purlwise (from those just cast on), purl to end – 70 sts.
**Row 2:** Skp, knit to end – 69 sts.
**Row 3:** Cast off 10 sts purlwise, purl to last 2 sts, p2tog – 58 sts.
**Row 4:** Knit.
**Row 5:** Cast off 43 sts purlwise, purl to last 2 sts, p2tog – 14 sts.
**Row 6:** Knit.
**Row 7:** Spp, purl to last 2 sts, p2tog – 12 sts.
**Rows 8 & 9:** Rep Rows 6 & 7 once – 10 sts.
**Row 10:** Skp, knit to last 2 sts, k2tog – 8 sts.
**Row 11:** Spp, purl to last 2 sts, p2tog – 6 sts.
Cast off knitwise.

### *For Pencil Case Only:*

Cut 2 pieces of interfacing the same shape as the left and right sides of body and iron to the WS of each body piece.

## HEAD GUSSET

Cast on 2 sts.

**Row 1 (RS):** Kfb, k1 – 3 sts.

Work 3 rows St st, beg with a purl row.

**Next row:** K1, m1, knit to last st, m1, k1 – 5 sts.

Work 7 rows St st, beg with a purl row.

**Next row:** K1, m1, knit to last st, m1, k1 – 7 sts.

Work straight in St st, beg with a purl row, until piece measures 8 cm (3¼ in), ending with a WS row.

**Next row:** Skp, knit to last 2 sts, k2tog – 5 sts.

Work 5 rows St st, beg with a purl row.

Rep last 6 rows once more – 3 sts.

**Next row:** Sk2p. Fasten off.

With WS facing, use tapestry needle to sew Head Gusset in place to top of head of left and right sides of body, placing cast-on point of gusset at nose.

Fold legs lengthways and sew side seams of legs, leaving feet open.

Sew 2 pieces of tail together lengthways.

## LEFT BODY GUSSET

With RS facing, pu and knit 7 sts along inside edge of Left Front Leg, 23 sts along cast-on edge of Left Side Body, then 6 sts along inside edge of Left Back Leg – 36 sts.

**Row 1 (WS):** Pfb, purl to last 2 sts, pfb, p1 – 38 sts.

**Row 2:** Kfb, knit to end – 39 sts.

Rep Rows 1 & 2 a further 4 times – 51 sts.

Break off yarn and place sts onto a stitch holder.

## RIGHT BODY GUSSET

With RS facing, pu and knit 6 sts along inside edge of Right Back Leg, 23 sts along cast-on edge of Right Side Body, then 7 sts along inside edge of Right Front Leg – 36 sts.

**Row 1 (WS):** Pfb, purl to last 2 sts, pfb, p1 – 38 sts.

**Row 2:** Knit to last 2 sts, kfb, k1 – 39 sts.

Rep Rows 1 & 2 a further 4 times – 51 sts.

### Join Body Gussets:

Place Left Body Gusset sts onto one needle so that point of needle is at head end of gusset.

With RS facing each other, hold needles of both body gusset pieces in left hand and then, using an extra needle, join using three-needle cast-off (see page 127) on WS.

Using tapestry needle, sew gusset to left and right sides of body along each side of chest and buttocks.
Sew lower seam of head and neck of both body pieces.

## LEFT OUTER & RIGHT INNER EARS (Make 2)

Cast on 4 sts.
**Row 1 (WS):** P2, pfb, p1 – 5 sts.
**Row 2:** Kfb, knit to end – 6 sts.
**Row 3:** Purl to last 2 sts, pfb, p1 – 7 sts.
**Row 4:** Kfb, knit to end – 8 sts.
Work 5 rows St st, beg with a purl row.
Rep last 6 rows twice more – 10 sts.
**Next row:** Skp, knit to end – 9 sts.
Cast off purlwise.

## LEFT INNER & RIGHT OUTER EARS (Make 2)

Cast on 4 sts.
**Row 1 (RS):** K2, kfb, k1 – 5 sts.
**Row 2:** Pfb, purl to end – 6 sts.
**Row 3:** Knit to last 2 sts, kfb, k1 – 7 sts.
**Row 4:** Pfb, purl to end – 8 sts.
Work 5 rows St st, beg with a knit row.
Rep last 6 rows twice more – 10 sts.
**Next row:** Spp, purl to end – 9 sts.
Cast off knitwise.

## FOOT PADS (Make 4)

Cast on 3 sts.
**Row 1 (WS):** Purl.
**Row 2:** [Kfb] into each of next 2 sts, k1 – 5 sts.
Work 5 rows St st, beg with a purl row.
**Next row:** Skp, k1, k2tog – 3 sts.
**Next row:** Sp2p. Fasten off.

## FINISHING

Using tapestry needle, weave in ends on WS.
Sew Foot Pads to ends of legs.
Fill legs and head with fibre filling.

## TOY ONLY

Fill body with fibre filling, then sew back seam.

## PENCIL CASE ONLY

Sew a small piece of lining fabric on the inside of body at top of leg and neck openings to hold filling in place.

Hem along both 22 cm (8 3/4 in) sides of lining fabric. Fold fabric with hemmed edge at top for zip opening and making a pleat 3.5 cm (1 1/2 in) deep at lower edge. Sew side edges of fabric, sewing folds of pleat in place. Insert lining into body and tack in place along opening, 1.5 cm (3/4 in) from edges.

Use a sewing needle and thread to sew zip into place between outer layer of opening and lining. Remove tacking stitches.

## TOY & PENCIL CASE

Sew ear pieces together in pairs, then sew cast-off edges in position along edges of head gusset, placing straight edge of ear towards front of head.

Thread tapestry needle with black yarn and embroider eyes and nose using satin st.

# Bird-of-Paradise Socks

The simple, geometric stitch pattern climbing up the sides of these socks resembles the flowers of one of my favourite plants.

## SIZES
Adult's small (medium:large)

## FINISHED MEASUREMENTS
Foot circumference:
19 (20.5: 23) cm [7½ (8:9) in]

Length of foot: 22 (24:26) cm
[8¾ (9½:10¼) in]

Length of leg (approx): 26.5 cm
[10½ in]

## YARN
Koigu Premium Merino KPM
[100% merino; 160 metres
(175 yards) / 50 grams]:
3 hanks #2355

## NEEDLES
Set of 2.5 mm double pointed

Set of 2.75 mm double pointed

Change needle size if necessary
to obtain correct tension.

## NOTIONS
5 stitch markers (1 in a contrasting
colour); tapestry needle; stitch
holder

## TENSION
32 sts and 46 rnds = 10 cm (4 in) in
stitch pattern using size 2.75 mm
needles

## STITCH PATTERN
(worked over 20 sts – 20 rnd rep)
**Rnd 1:** K10, p10.
**Rnd 2:** K10, p9, k1.
**Rnd 3:** K10, p8, k2.
**Rnd 4:** K10, p7, k3.
**Rnd 5:** K10, p6, k4.
**Rnd 6:** K10, p5, k5.
**Rnd 7:** K10, p4, k6.
**Rnd 8:** K10, p3, k7.
**Rnd 9:** K10, p2, k8.
**Rnd 10:** K10, p1, k9.
**Rnd 11:** P10, k10.
**Rnd 12:** K1, p9, k10.
**Rnd 13:** K2, p8, k10.
**Rnd 14:** K3, p7, k10.
**Rnd 15:** K4, p6, k10.
**Rnd 16:** K5, p5, k10.
**Rnd 17:** K6, p4, k10.
**Rnd 18:** K7, p3, k10.
**Rnd 19:** K8, p2, k10.
**Rnd 20:** K9, p1, k10.
Rep Rnds 1–20 for Stitch Pattern.

## SOCK (Make 2)

With smaller dpns, cast on 72 (76:84) sts, dividing sts evenly over 3 needles.
Join for working in the rnd, being careful not to twist sts; pcm for beg of rnd and sm on every rnd.
**Rnd 1:** *K1, p1; rep from * to end.
Rep Rnd 1 until piece measures 5 cm (2 in) from beg.
Change to larger dpns.

**Next rnd:** K8 (9:11), pm, k20, pm, k16 (18:22), pm, k20, pm, k8 (9:11).

Commence Stitch Patt as foll:

**Rnd 1 (RS):** *K8 (9:11), sm, work first row of Stitch Patt over next 20 sts, sm, k8 (9:11); rep from * to end.

Slipping markers on every rnd, cont working Stitch Patt between markers as established, with St st either side, as foll: Work 6 rnds.

### Shape Leg:

**Rnd 8:** [Knit to 2 sts before marker, ssk, sm, work 20 sts, sm, k2tog] twice, knit to end – 68 (72:80) sts.

Dec 1 st (as before) either side of Stitch Patt in every foll 18th rnd twice – 60 (64:72) sts.

Work until 20 rnds of Stitch Patt have been completed a total of 5 times, removing patt markers in last rnd.

### Heel Flap:

**Next row:** K15 (16:18), turn.

**Next row:** P30 (32:36), turn.

Work back and forth in rows on these 30 (32:36) sts only, leaving rem 30 (32:36) sts on a stitch holder for instep.

**Row 1 (RS):** *Slip 1 purlwise wyib, k1; rep from * to end.

**Row 2:** Slip 1 purlwise wyif, purl to end.

Rep Rows 1 & 2 a further 14 (15:16) times.

### Turn Heel:

**Row 1 (RS):** K17 (18:20), ssk, k1, turn.

**Row 2:** Slip 1 purlwise wyif, p5, p2tog, p1, turn.

**Row 3:** Slip 1 purlwise wyib, k6, ssk, k1, turn.

**Row 4:** Slip 1 purlwise wyif, p7, p2tog, p1, turn.

**Row 5:** Slip 1 purlwise wyib, k8, ssk, k1, turn.

**Row 6:** Slip 1 purlwise wyif, p9, p2tog, p1, turn.

**Row 7:** Slip 1 purlwise wyib, k10, ssk, k1, turn.

**Row 8:** Slip 1 purlwise wyif, p11, p2tog, p1, turn.

**Row 9:** Slip 1 purlwise wyib, k12, ssk, k1, turn.

**Row 10:** Slip 1 purlwise wyif, p13, p2tog, p1, turn.

**Row 11:** Slip 1 purlwise wyib, k14, ssk, k1, turn.

**Row 12:** Slip 1 purlwise wyif, p15, p2tog, p1, turn – 18 (20:24) sts.

### Size Medium Only:

**Row 13:** Slip 1 purlwise wyib, k16, ssk, turn.

**Row 14:** Slip 1 purlwise wyif, p16, p2tog, turn – 18 sts.

*Size Large Only:*
**Row 13:** Slip 1 purlwise wyib, k16, ssk, k1, turn.
**Row 14:** Slip 1 purlwise wyif, p17, p2tog, p1, turn.
**Row 15:** Slip 1 purlwise wyib, k18, ssk, turn.
**Row 16:** Slip 1 purlwise wyif, p18, p2tog, turn – 20 sts.

*All Sizes:*
18 (18:20) sts.
(All heel sts have now been worked).

**Gusset and Foot:**
Knit heel sts with same dpn (needle 1), then using same
needle pu and knit 16 (17:18) sts along selvedge edge of heel
flap; with second dpn (needle 2), knit across 30 (32:36) instep
sts from stitch holder; with a third dpn (needle 3), pu and knit
16 (17:18) sts along other selvedge edge of heel flap, then knit
across first 9 (9:10) heel sts – 80 (84:92) sts [25 (26:28) sts on
each of needles 1 & 3 and 30 (32:36) sts on needle 2].
Rnd now begins at centre back heel.
**Rnd 1:** Knit to last 3 sts, k2tog, k1 from needle 1; knit instep sts
from needle 2; k1, ssk, knit to end from needle 3 – 78 (82:90) sts.
**Rnd 2:** Knit.
Rep Rnds 1 & 2 until 60 (64:72) sts rem.
Work straight until foot measures 17.5 (19:20.5) cm
[7 (7½:8) in] or approx 4.5 (5:5.5) cm [1¾ (2:2¼) in]
less than desired foot length.

**Shape Toe:**
**Rnd 1:** Knit to last 3 sts, k2tog, k1 from needle 1; k1, ssk, knit
to last 3 sts, k2tog, k1 from needle 2; k1, ssk, knit to end from
needle 3 – 56 (60:68) sts.
**Rnd 2:** Knit.
Rep Rnds 1 & 2 until 32 (32:40) sts rem, then rep Rnd 1 only until
12 sts rem.
Knit sts from needle 1 onto needle 3 (there will be 6 sts on
each of two needles).
Break off yarn, leaving a 45 cm (18 in) tail and thread onto
tapestry needle.
Graft sts together on RS using Kitchener Stitch (see page 126).
Weave in ends on WS.

# Airplane Socks

Because I have to travel so far from New Zealand to visit my family, I wanted to make a pair of comfy socks to wear on the airplane once I kick off my shoes and settle in for a long flight. These are made of organic cotton and would look adorable worn with shoes, too. To make a longer sock, work the picot edging and then a longer ribbing before beginning the heel shaping.

## SIZE
Women's small (medium:large)

## FINISHED MEASUREMENTS
Foot circumference:
19 (20.5:21.5) cm [7½ (8:8½) in]

Length of foot: 22 (24:26) cm
[8¾ (9½:10¼) in]

## YARN
Rowan Purelife Organic Cotton Naturally Dyed [100% organic cotton; 165 metres (180 yards) / 50 grams]: 2 skeins #751 natural

## NEEDLES
Set of 2.75 mm double pointed

Set of 3.25 mm double pointed

Change needle size if necessary to obtain correct tension.

## NOTIONS
3 stitch markers (1 in a contrasting colour); stitch holder; tapestry needle

## TENSION
28 sts and 36 rnds = 10 cm (4 in) in St st using size 3.25 mm needles

## SOCK (Make 2)

(Commence at ankle)

With smaller dpns, cast on 108 (108:120) sts, dividing evenly over 3 needles.

Join for working in the rnd, being careful not to twist sts; pcm for beg of rnd and sm on every rnd.

**Rnd 1:** K1, *Cast off next 3 sts, k3 (including st on right needle after casting off); rep from * ending last rep k2 instead of k3 – 54 (54:60) sts.

**Rnd 2:** *K1, p1; rep from * to end.

Rep Rnd 2 a further 4 (4:5) times.

### Sizes Small and Medium only:
Rep Rnd 2 once more, dec (inc) 2 sts evenly across last rnd – 52 (56) sts.

### All Sizes:
52 (56:60) sts.

Change to larger dpns.

### Heel Flap:
**Next row:** K13 (14:15), turn.

**Next row:** P26 (28:30), turn.

Work back and forth in rows on these 26 (28:30) sts only, leaving rem 26 (28:30) sts on a stitch holder for instep.

**Row 1 (RS):** *Slip 1 purlwise wyib, k1; rep from * to end.

**Row 2:** Slip 1 purlwise wyif, purl to end.

Rep Rows 1 & 2 a further 12 (13:14) times.

### Turn Heel:
**Row 1 (RS):** K15 (16:17), ssk, k1, turn.

**Row 2:** Slip 1 purlwise wyif, p5, p2tog, p1, turn.

**Row 3:** Slip 1 purlwise wyib, k6, ssk, k1, turn.

**Row 4:** Slip 1 purlwise wyif, p7, p2tog, p1, turn.

**Row 5:** Slip 1 purlwise wyib, k8, ssk, k1, turn.
**Row 6:** Slip 1 purlwise wyif, p9, p2tog, p1, turn.
**Row 7:** Slip 1 purlwise wyib, k10, ssk, k1, turn.
**Row 8:** Slip 1 purlwise wyif, p11, p2tog, p1, turn.
**Row 9:** Slip 1 purlwise wyib, k12, ssk, k1, turn.
**Row 10:** Slip 1 purlwise wyif, p13, p2tog, p1, turn – 16 (18:20) sts.

*Size Medium Only:*
**Row 11:** Slip 1 purlwise wyib, k14, ssk, turn.
**Row 12:** Slip 1 purlwise wyif, p14, p2tog, turn – 16 sts.

*Size Large Only:*
**Row 11:** Slip 1 purlwise wyib, k14, ssk, k1, turn.
**Row 12:** Slip 1 purlwise wyif, p15, p2tog, p1, turn – 18 sts.

*All Sizes:*
16 (16:18) sts (all heel sts have now been worked).

**Gusset and Foot:**
Knit heel sts with same dpn (needle 1), then using same needle pu and knit 14 (15:16) sts along selvedge edge of heel flap; with a second dpn (needle 2), knit across 26 (28:30) instep sts from stitch holder; with a third dpn (needle 3), pu and knit 14 (15:16) sts along other selvedge edge of heel flap, then knit across first 8 (8:9) heel sts – 70 (74:80) sts [22 (23:25) sts on each of needles 1 & 3 and 26 (28:30) sts on needle 2].
Rnd now begins at centre back heel.
**Rnd 1:** Knit to last 3 sts, k2tog, k1 from needle 1; knit instep sts from needle 2; k1, ssk, knit to end from needle 3 – 68 (72:78) sts.
**Rnd 2:** Knit.
Rep Rnds 1 & 2 twice more, then Rnd 1 once – 62 (66:72) sts.
**Rnd 8:** Knit sts from needle 1; k7 (8:9), pm, k12, pm, k7 (8:9) from needle 2; knit to end of needle 3.

*Commence working from chart as foll:*
**Rnd 1:** Knit to last 2 sts, k2tog, k1 from needle 1; k7 (8:9), sm, k10, k2tog, yo, sm, k7 (8:9) from needle 2; ssk, knit to end of needle 3 – 60 (64:70) sts.
Slipping markers in every rnd, cont working chart between markers as established, with St st either side, as foll:
Dec 1 st (as before) on each of needles 1 & 3 on every foll alt rnd until 52 (56:60) sts rem.
Work straight until foot measures approx 17 (19:21) cm [6¾ (7½:8¼) in] or approx 5 cm (2 in) less than desired foot length, ending with either Rnd 11 or Rnd 15 of chart and removing chart markers in last rnd.

## Shape Toe:

**Rnd 1:** Knit to last 3 sts, k2tog, k1 from needle 1; k1, ssk, knit to last 3 sts, k2tog, k1 from needle 2; k1, ssk, knit to end of needle 3 – 48 (52:56) sts.

**Rnd 2:** Knit.

Rep Rnds 1 & 2 until 24 (28:28) sts rem, then rep Rnd 1 only until 8 sts rem.

Knit sts from needle 1 onto needle 3 (there will be 4 sts on each of two needles).

Break off yarn, leaving a 45 cm (18 in) tail and thread onto tapestry needle.

Graft sts together on RS using Kitchener Stitch (see page 126)

Weave in ends on WS.

## CHART

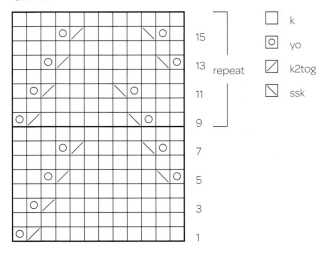

repeat

| | |
|---|---|
| ☐ | k |
| ⊡ | yo |
| ◪ | k2tog |
| ◩ | ssk |

## NOTE

When working from the chart, read all rnds from right to left.

# Tangerine Tights

Caitlyn, one of our models, arrived at the shoot wearing a pair of her Mum's 1960s tights. Glimpses are seen in the photos, so I decided to include a pattern for them, just in case someone reading this book might want to make a pair of wool tights! Knitting them was quite a marathon, but well worth the effort because they're very comfortable. I'm several sizes larger than the model in the photo, but they fit me because there is so much ease in the ribbing. They're worked from the toe up, and must be tried on at intervals to ensure adequate leg length.

## FINISHED MEASUREMENTS

Foot circumference: 15–25.5 cm (6–10 in); Calf circumference: 15–35.5 cm (6–14 in); Thigh circumference: 20.5–61 cm (8–24 in); Waist circumference: 51–102 cm (20–40¼ in)

## YARN

Koigu Premium Merino KPM [100% merino; 160 metres (175 yards) / 50 grams]: 8 hanks #2355 (A).
*Yarn amount is for an inner leg length (heel to top of thigh when worn) of 80 cm (31½ in).*

## NEEDLES

Set of 2.75 mm double pointed

2.75 mm x 80 cm (32 in) circular

## NOTIONS

4 stitch markers; spare yarn; 2.5 cm (1 in) wide elastic to fit comfortably around waist; sewing needle and thread; tapestry needle

## TENSION

30 sts and 46 rnds = 10 cm (4 in) in St st using size 2.75 mm needles

50 sts and 40 rnds = 10 cm (4 in) in 2x2 rib using size 2.75 mm needles

## RIGHT LEG

### Toe Section:

With spare yarn and 2 dpns, cast on 30 sts. Change to A, working back and forth in rows as foll:

**Row 1 (WS):** Purl.

**\*\* Row 2:** Knit to last st, wrap, turn.

**Row 3:** Purl to last st, wrap, turn.

**Row 4:** Knit to 1 st before last wrapped st, wrap, turn.

**Row 5:** Purl to 1 st before last wrapped st, wrap, turn.

Rep Rows 4 & 5 until there are 12 sts between wrapped sts.

**Next row (RS):** Slip 1 knitwise, knit to next wrapped st, knit next st and wrap together, turn.

**Next row:** Slip 1 purlwise, purl to next wrapped st, purl next st and wrap together, turn.

Rep last 2 rows until all sts have been worked. \*\*

### Foot Gusset:

Carefully remove spare yarn from cast-on row and slip these 30 sts evenly over 2 dpns – 60 sts [30 sts on needle 1; 15 sts on each of needles 2 & 3].

Work in rnds over all sts as foll:

**Rnd 1:** Needle 1: K32 [p2, k2] 7 times.

Rep Rnd 1 until foot measures 19 cm (7½ in), or 5 cm (2 in) less than desired foot length.

### Shape Heel:

Work as for Toe Section from \*\* to \*\*, working back and forth over 30 sts on needle 1 only.

## Commence Leg:

With RS facing, sl 1 knitwise, k29, pu and knit 2 sts in corner of heel, [k2, p2] 7 times, k2, pu and knit 2 sts in corner of heel – 64 sts.

**Next rnd:** [K2, p2] 15 times, k2, p1, slide next (purl) st onto needle 1 [32 sts on needle 1, 16 sts on each of needles 2 & 3]. Work in 2x2 rib as set until Leg measures 61 cm (24 in) from heel. \*\*\*\*

## Shape Inner Thigh:

**Next rnd:** P1, [k2, p2] 3 times, k2, [p1, m1p, p1, k2] 8 times, [p2, k2] 4 times, p1 – 72 sts.
**Next rnd:** P1, [k2, p2] 3 times, k2, [p3, k2] 8 times, [p2, k2] 4 times, p1.
Rep last rnd until leg is 15 cm (6 in) less than desired length of Inner Thigh.

## Shape Outer Thigh:

**Next rnd:** M1p, p1, [k2, p1, m1p, p1] 3 times, [k2, p3] 8 times, k2, p1, [m1p, p1, k2, p1] 4 times – 80 sts.
**Next rnd:** P2, k2, \*p3, k2; rep from \* to last st, p1.
Work 7.5 cm (3 in) in k2, p3 rib as established.

## Shape Upper Thigh:

**Next rnd:** P2, [k1, m1, k1, p3] 15 times, k1, m1, k1, p1 – 96 sts.
Work 7.5 cm (3 in) in k3, p3 rib as established.

## Shape Gusset:

**Next rnd:** Rib 48, pm, m1, k1, m1, pm, rib to end – 98 sts.
**Next rnd:** Rib to marker, sm, knit to marker, sm, rib to end.
**Next rnd:** Rib to marker, sm, m1, knit to marker, m1, sm, rib to end – 100 sts.
Rep last 2 rnds once more – 102 sts [7 sts between markers].
**Next rnd:** Rib to marker, sm, knit to marker, sm, rib to end.
Place sts and markers onto a holding thread.

## LEFT LEG

Work as for Right Leg to \*\*\*\*.

## Shape Inner Thigh:

**Next rnd:** M1p, p1, [k2, p1, m1p, p1] 4 times, [k2, p2] 8 times, [k2, p1, m1p, p1] 3 times, k2, p1 – 72 sts.
**Next rnd:** P2, [k2, p3] 4 times, [k2, p2] 8 times, [k2, p3] 3 times, k2, p1.
Rep last rnd until leg is 15 cm (6 in) less than desired length of Inner Thigh.

**NOTE**

Since length when worn varies according to circumference of calf and thigh, it is necessary to try on for size.

## Shape Outer Thigh:

**Next rnd:** P2, [k2, p3] 4 times, k2, [p1, m1p, p1, k2] 8 times, [p3, k2] 3 times, p1 – 80 sts.
**Next rnd:** P2, k2, *p3, k2; rep from * to last st, p1.
Work 7.5 cm (3 in) in k2, p3 rib as established.

## Shape Upper Thigh:

**Next rnd:** P2, [k1, m1, k1, p3] 15 times, k1, m1, k1, p1 – 96 sts.
Work 7.5 cm (3 in) in k3, p3 rib as established.

## Shape Gusset:

**Next rnd:** Pm, m1, k1, m1, pm, rib to end – 98 sts.
**Next rnd:** Sm, knit to marker, sm, rib to end.
**Next rnd:** Sm, m1, knit to marker, m1, sm, rib to end – 100 sts.
Rep last 2 rnds once more – 102 sts [7 sts between markers].
**Next rnd:** Sm, knit to marker, sm, rib to end.
Do not break off yarn.
Place sts and markers onto a holding thread.

# GUSSET INSERT (MAKE 2)

With spare yarn and 2 dpns, cast on 10 sts.
Change to A.
**Row 1 (RS):** Knit.
Break off yarn and set aside.

# PANTIE

## Join Legs:

With circular needle, RS facing and beginning at Left Leg Gusset, sm, knit first 3 sts from gusset, k10 sts of first Gusset Insert, knit last 3 sts of Right Leg Gusset, sm, rib across all Right Leg sts to marker, sm, knit rem 4 gusset sts, k10 sts of second Gusset Insert, knit rem 4 sts from Left Leg Gusset, rib across all Left Leg sts to marker – 224 sts.
There will be 16 gusset sts at front and 18 gusset sts at back.
Work 8 rnds straight in rib, working gusset sts in St st.

## Shape Gusset:

**Next rnd:** [Sm, ssk, knit to 2 sts before marker, k2tog, sm, rib to next marker] twice – 220 sts.
Cont in rib and St st as established, dec 1 st (as before) at each end of gussets on every foll 3rd rnd three times, then on every foll alt rnd three times – 196 sts.
**Next rnd:** Sm, skp, sm, rib to next marker, sm, ssk, k2tog, sm, rib to end – 193 sts.

**Next rnd:** Sm, p1, remove marker, rib to next marker, remove marker, skp, remove marker, rib to end – 192 sts.
**Next rnd:** Sm, p2, k3, *p3, k3; rep from * to last st, p1.
Cont in k3, p3 rib as established until pantie measures to lower waist when tights are worn. Work a further 4 cm (1½ in) in rib.
Cast off loosely ribwise.

## FINISHING

Remove spare yarn from gusset sts and with RS facing, join using Kitchener Stitch (see page 126). Turn tights inside out.
Using tapestry needle, weave in ends on WS.
Turn top of pantie over and use tapestry needle to sew into place on WS, allowing depth for 2.5 cm (1 in) elastic to be inserted and leaving a space in waistband for elastic to be threaded through.
Cut a length of elastic slightly smaller than waist measurement. Thread elastic through waistband and use sewing needle and thread to sew ends together.
Using tapestry needle, sew remainder of hem.

# SUBSTITUTING YARNS

I have tried to use a selection of yarns that are widely available. The three New Zealand yarns I have used may not be available in the UK, but others can be easily substituted.

A local yarn shop cannot possibly stock every yarn that exists and there are yarns that are available in some countries and not others. Many are available online. I would encourage knitters to buy from their local shop whenever possible. Shop owners provide a valuable service and need to be supported.

If your local shop doesn't have a yarn you're looking for, here are some guidelines for yarn substitution.

*There are a few considerations when deciding what yarns to use.*

### Needle size
Look at the needle size used in the pattern. This will give you an idea of the weight of yarn used. Look also at whether the yarn is used single, or if it might be used multi-stranded.

### Quantity
Always calculate quantities by looking at how many metres or yards are in each skein, not at the gram weight. Some fibres are heavier than others and will have different lengths per gram. Most yarn labels include this information.

### Yarns
To the right is a list of the yarns I used for the projects, and their rating according to the Standard Yarn Weight System on page 123, which you can use to compare yarns.

I have also listed the websites for the yarn companies which, in most cases, display a list of their retail stockists.

Koigu KPPPM & KPM  [1]
**www.koigu.com**

Cascade 220  [3]
Cascade Ecological Wool [5]
**www.cascadeyarns.com**

Blue Sky Alpacas Worsted Cotton [4]
Blue Sky Alpacas Worsted [5]
Blue Sky Alpaca Silk [2]
**www.blueskyalpacas.com**

Spud & Chloë Sweater Superwash  [3]
**www.spudandchloe.com**

Manos Del Uruguay Wool Clasica [4]
**www.manos.com.uy**

Rowan Kidsilk Haze [2]
Rowan Purelife Organic Cotton [1]
Rowan Wool Cotton [2]
**www.knitrowan.com**

The Fibre Company Terra [4]
**www.thefibreco.com**

Naturally Lace  [0]
Naturally Heather [3]
Naturally Loyal [3]
**www.naturallyyarnsnz.com**

Jade Sapphire Mongolian Cashmere 8 ply [4]
**www.jadesapphire.com**

# STANDARD YARN WEIGHT SYSTEM

Categories of yarn, tension ranges and recommended needle sizes
Source: Adapted from the Craft Yarn Council's www.YarnStandards.com

| YARN WEIGHT SYMBOL & CATEGORY NAMES | TYPE OF YARNS IN CATEGORY | KNIT TENSION* IN ST ST TO 10 CM | RECOMMENDED NEEDLE SIZE |
|---|---|---|---|
| **0** LACE | Fingering 10-count crochet thread | 33—40** sts | 1.5—2.25 mm |
| **1** SUPER FINE | Sock, Fingering, Baby | 27—32 sts | 2.25—3.25 mm |
| **2** FINE | Sport, Baby | 23—26 sts | 3.25—3.75 mm |
| **3** LIGHT | DK, Light Worsted | 21—24 st | 3.75—4.5 mm |
| **4** MEDIUM | Worsted, Afghan, Aran | 16—20 sts | 4.5—5.5 mm |
| **5** BULKY | Chunky, Craft, Rug | 12—15 sts | 5.5—8 mm |

\* Guidelines only: the above reflect the most commonly used tensions and needle sizes for specific yarn categories.

\*\* Lace-weight yarns are usually knitted on larger needles to create lacy, openwork patterns. Accordingly, a tension range is difficult to determine. Always follow the tension stated in your pattern.

# ABBREVIATIONS

| | |
|---|---|
| Alt | Alternate |
| Approx | Approximately |
| Beg | Begin(ning) |
| Cm | Centimetres |
| Cn | Cable needle |
| Cont | Continue(d) |
| Dec | Decrease(ing) |
| Dpn(s) | Double pointed needle(s) |
| Foll | Follow(s)(ing) |
| Inc | Increase(ing) |
| In | Inch(es) |
| K | Knit |
| K2tog | Knit 2 sts together. |
| K2tog tbl | Knit 2 sts together through back of loops. |
| Kfb | Knit into front and then back of next st. |
| M1 or M1l (left slanting increase) | With the tip of the left needle inserted from front to back, lift the strand between the two needles onto the left needle; knit the strand through the back of the loop to twist the st. |
| M1p or M1pl (left slanting increase purlwise) | With the tip of the left needle inserted from back to front, lift the strand between the two needles onto the left needle; purl the strand through the front of the loop to twist the st. |
| M1pr (right slanting increase purlwise) | With the tip of the left needle inserted from front to back, lift the strand between the two needles onto the left needle; purl the strand through the back of the loop to twist the st. |

| | |
|---|---|
| M1r (right slanting increase) | With the tip of the left needle inserted from back to front, lift the strand between the two needles onto the left needle; knit the strand through the front of the loop to twist the st. |
| Mm | Millimetres |
| 0 | No rows/stitches/times |
| P | Purl |
| P2tog | Purl 2 sts together. |
| P2tog tbl | Purl 2 sts together through back of loops. |
| Patt | Pattern |
| Pcm | Place contrasting marker |
| Pfb | Purl into front and then back of next st. |
| Pm | Place marker |
| Psso | Pass the slipped st over the last st. |
| Pu | Pick up |
| Rem | Remain(ing) |
| Rep | Repeat |
| Rnd(s) | Round(s) |
| RS | Right side |
| Skp | Slip 1 st knitwise to right-hand needle, k1, pass the slipped st over the knit st. |
| Sk2p | Slip 1 st knitwise to right-hand needle, k2tog, pass the slipped st over st from k2tog. |
| Sl | Slip |
| Sm | Slip marker |
| Sp2p | Slip 1 st purlwise to right-hand needle, p2tog, pass the slipped st over st from p2tog. |

| | | | |
|---|---|---|---|
| **Spp** | Slip 1 st purlwise to right-hand needle, purl next st, pass the slipped st over the purl st. | **Tog** | Together |
| | | **Wyib** | With yarn in back |
| | | **Wyif** | With yarn in front |
| | | **WS** | Wrong side |
| **Ssk** | Slip next 2 sts knitwise to right-hand needle one at a time, insert left needle into sts and knit together. | **Yb** | Yarn back |
| | | **Yf** | Yarn front |
| | | **Yo** | Yarn over needle |
| **St(s)** | Stitch(es) | | |
| **St st** | Stocking stitch (knit all rnds; or RS row knit, WS row purl) | | |
| **Tbl** | Through back of loop | | |

# TECHNIQUES

### CABLE CAST-ON (Knitwise)

Leaving a 30 cm (12 in) tail, make a slip knot in the yarn and place it on left needle (this is the first stitch cast on). Knit into the slip knot, drawing up a loop (as if to knit) and place the new loop on left needle; *insert the tip of the right needle into the space between the last 2 stitches on left needle, wrap the yarn around the needle as if to knit and draw up a loop; place loop on left needle. Repeat from * for remaining stitches to be cast on, or for casting on at the beginning of a row.

### CABLE CAST-ON (Purlwise)

Leaving a 30 cm (12 in) tail, make a slip knot in the yarn and place it on left needle (this is the first stitch cast on). Purl into the slip knot, drawing up a loop (as if to purl) and place the new loop on left needle; *insert the tip of the right needle into the space between the last 2 stitches on left needle from behind, wrap the yarn around the needle as if to purl and draw up a loop; place loop on left needle. Repeat from * for remaining stitches to be cast on, or for casting on at the beginning of a row.

### FELTING

Wash item in hot water and lanolin soap in a washing machine with a towel for friction. Depending on the temperature of the water, you may need to repeat the washing process two or three times for item to felt adequately and become firm enough. Stuff with paper (to keep desired shape) and set aside to dry naturally.

### KITCHENER STITCH

Thread a length of yarn approximately 4 times the length of the section to be joined onto tapestry needle. Hold the pieces to be joined in left hand, with needles parallel and either right sides together or wrong sides together, as indicated in pattern. Working from right to left, insert tapestry needle into first stitch on front needle as if to purl, pull yarn through, leaving stitch on the needle; insert tapestry needle into first stitch on back needle as if to knit, pull yarn through, leaving stitch on the needle; **insert tapestry needle into first stitch on front needle as if to knit, pull yarn through, remove stitch from needle, insert tapestry needle into next stitch on front needle as if to purl, pull yarn through, leave stitch on needle; insert tapestry needle into first stitch on back needle as if to purl, pull yarn through, remove stitch from needle, insert tapestry needle into next stitch on back needle as if to knit, pull yarn through, leave stitch on needle; repeat from **, working 3 or 4 stitches at a time, then go back and adjust tension to match pieces being joined. When 1 stitch remains on each needle, break off yarn and pass through last 2 stitches to fasten off.

## KITCHENER STITCH FOR 1X1 RIB

With right sides facing, transfer all knit stitches from each piece to be joined onto separate needles, ensuring that points of both needles are facing in the same direction. With right sides facing, hold the knit stitches of the two sections together with needles pointing to the right, then join using Kitchener Stitch (page 126). Transfer the held purl stitches (they will be knit stitches on the wrong side) from each piece onto separate needles, ensuring that points of both needles are facing in the same direction. With wrong sides facing, hold the stitches of the two sections together with needles pointing to the right, then join using Kitchener Stitch (page 126).

## THREE-NEEDLE CAST-OFF

Place the stitches to be joined onto two same-sized needles; hold the pieces to be joined with the right or wrong sides facing each other, as indicated in the pattern, and the needles parallel, both pointing to the right. Holding both needles in your left hand, using working yarn and a third needle the same size, insert third needle into back of first stitch on front needle, then into front of first stitch on back needle; knit these 2 stitches together; *knit next stitch from each needle together in the same way (there will be 2 stitches on right needle); pass first stitch over second stitch to cast off 1 stitch. Repeat from * until 1 stitch remains on third needle; break off yarn and fasten off.

## WRAP

Bring yarn between the needles to other side of work, slide first stitch on left needle onto right needle purlwise, take yarn between the needles back to original side of work, slide wrapped stitch back to left needle, then continue as instructed. When next working over wrapped stitch, work the wrap and wrapped stitch together to prevent wrap from showing on RS of work.

# ACKNOWLEDGEMENTS

I spent several months working alone on this book, but when my spirits flagged and my deadline loomed, I was grateful for a few friends whose help I relied on.

My husband David makes me laugh, encourages me and generously tolerates my obsession. I rely on his opinions and taste and he often reminds me that there is beauty in simplicity. My wonderful kids, Pete and India, who spent their childhoods wearing hand knits without complaint, inspire me and give excellent advice on all matters knitting and otherwise.

Although I knitted most of the projects myself, I was grateful to be able to call on Marian Cox, Sally Duncan, Nicky Gray and Kirsten Brown for help with garments and extra colourways. Thank you to the models Nikau Hindin, Amelia MacDonald, Rikihana, Caitlyn Cook, Huia Minogue and India Wray-Murane. Many thanks to the Harres, who generously allowed us to photograph on their property at Oratia, Dave serving us bowls of hot soup and Barbara catching the chicken after we all tried and gave up because we were afraid of slipping in the mud. Thank you to Leanne Yare and Carolyn Haslett for letting us use their homes and to Erin and Darran at Madder and Rouge for opening early one morning so that we could take photographs in their beautiful shop.

I am grateful to Tracey Islè, who did the tech editing, and Therese Chynoweth, who drew the charts and schematics and did a final read-through of the patterns.

For pulling it all together, thank you to Xanthe Harrison, and to Tracey Borgfeldt for finding a way to write a knitting book in New Zealand.

Special thanks to Helen Bankers for her beautiful photographs and creativity.

*Thank you to the following businesses for letting me use their clothing and props:*

www.dalston.co.nz
www.flotsamandjetsam.co.nz
www.madderandrouge.co.nz
www.marvelmenswear.co.nz
www.minniecooper.co.nz
www.romantique.co.nz
www.starfish.co.nz
www.unodesign.co.nz
www.vanillaink.co.nz
www.widdess.co.nz